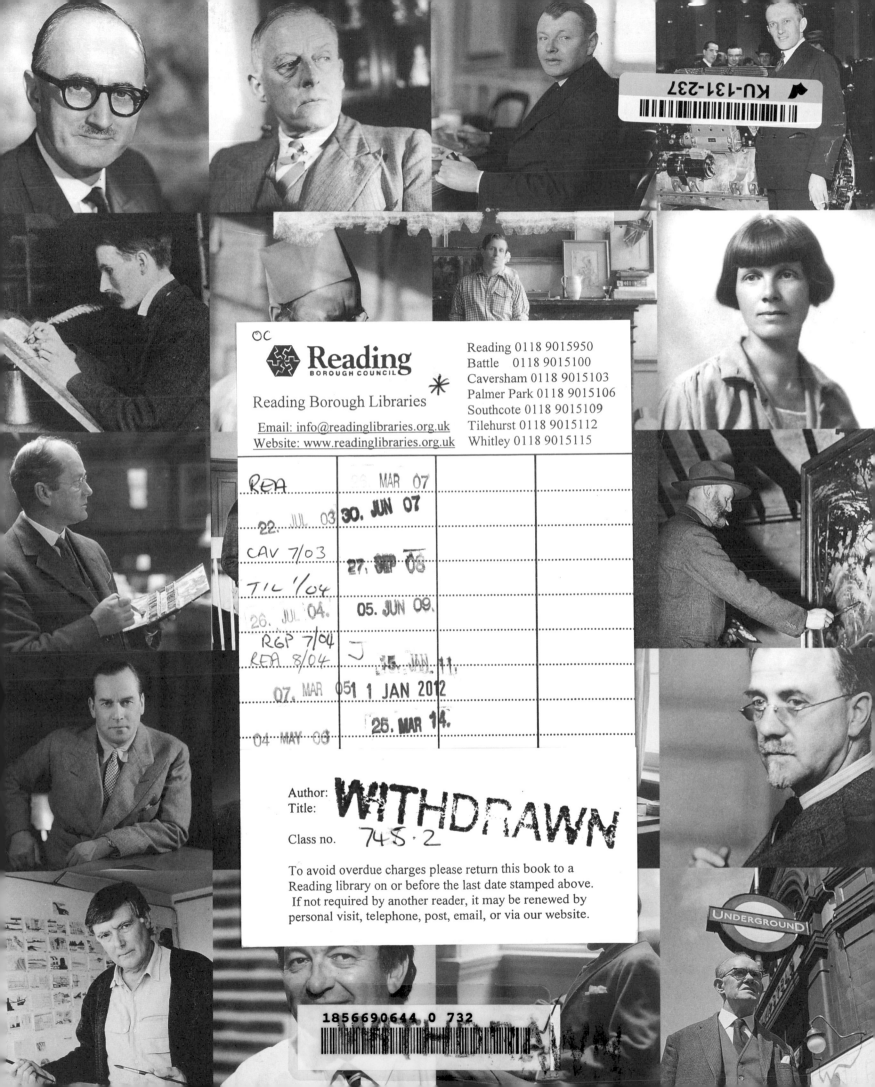

Designed for London

150 Years of
Transport Design

Designed for London

150 Years of Transport Design

Oliver Green and
Jeremy Rewse-Davies

Laurence King

Published 1995 by Laurence King Publishing
Copyright © 1995 London Transport Museum

A catalogue record for this book is available from the British
Library.

ISBN 1 85669 064 4

Designed by Pentagram, London
Printed in Singapore

Frontispiece: Stratford bus station by London Transport Bus
Passenger Infrastructure Architects.

Acknowledgements

Many people have contributed unknowingly to this book with
helpful ideas and information passed on to the authors over
many years. These include current and former employees of
London Transport and a number of the artists, designers and
architects who have carried out commissions of various kinds
for the organisation. We cannot credit them all individually,
but would like to thank by name those who have been directly
instrumental in the book's preparation. The authors are
particularly grateful to Marcia Morrison for typing the text
and captions, Sheila Taylor and Hugh Robertson of the
London Transport Museum Photo Library for researching and
providing photographs and Paul Castle, former Commercial
Manager of the London Transport Museum for securing the
publishing agreement on a project that has been on our wish
list for a very long time.

Photographic Credits

Most of the historic photographs in this book are from the
London Transport Museum Photo Library. New photographs
are from London Transport. We are grateful to the following
additional sources for allowing reproduction of their material:

Elizabeth Argent	Endpapers 37
Associated Electrical Industries Ltd	Endpapers 15
Stefan Buzas/RSA	Endpapers 6
Civil Engineering Department Library: History Collection, Imperial College, London	Endpapers 8
Design Council	Endpapers 9, 10
Ken Garland	Endpapers 40
Fay Godwin	Endpapers 25
Greater London Record Office Photo Collection	Endpapers 17
Holburne Museum and Crafts Study Centre, Bath	Endpapers 22
Courtesy of National Portrait Gallery, London	Endpapers 3, 11, 12, 16, 23, 24, 27, 28 (by Felix Man), 31, 32, 34, 35
Royal Society of Arts	Endpapers 2, 18, 19
Mrs Vera Stubbs/David Lawrence	Endpapers 33
Janine Weidel	Endpapers 20
Welch and Lander	p.133 lower right
The Worshipful Company of Goldsmiths	Endpapers 26
F. R. Yerbury – Architectural Association	p.123 lower and 126 lower left

Contents

Preface

This book is dedicated to the spirit of Frank Pick, the man who put good design at the heart of London Transport.

Pick was born in Spalding, Lincolnshire in 1878 and educated at St Peter's School, York. He qualified as a solicitor in 1902 and joined the North Eastern Railway as a management trainee. In 1906 he moved to London to work for the Underground Group. When Albert Stanley (later Lord Ashfield) arrived as General Manager the following year, Pick joined his office and was soon put in charge of publicity. It was a field in which he had no experience or qualifications, but it gave Pick his first opportunities in what would today be called design management.

As Pick rose through the Underground Group, his responsibilities broadened. He became, successively, Traffic Officer (1909), Commercial Manager (1912), Joint Assistant Managing Director (1921) and Managing Director (1928). When London Transport was created in 1933, Lord Ashfield was made the first Chairman of the Board, with Pick as Vice Chairman and Chief Executive. This 'formidable pair', as the Labour politician Herbert Morrison described them, were the driving force behind London Transport in the 1930s. Pick left in 1940 and was briefly Director General of the wartime Ministry of Information. He died in 1941.

Pick's passionate and crusading interest in design extended to many areas outside his career as a transport manager. He was a founder member of the Design and Industries Association, which was formed in 1915 to encourage better standards of commercial and industrial design, and became its president in 1932. In 1934 he was made the first Chairman of the Council for Art and Industry, forerunner of the present Design Council.

Pick applied the DIA's slogan 'fitness for purpose' more vigorously and effectively than any other leading commercial manager of his day. His tireless and thoughtful advocacy of the highest design standards make him one of the most important and influential figures in British design history.

Frank Pick (1878–1941), first Chief Executive of London Transport and the architect of the organisation's design philosophy. Pick had an almost visionary belief in London Transport's role, seeing it as far more than a mechanism for moving people around the capital: 'Underneath all the commercial activities of the Board, underneath all its engineering and operation, there is the revelation and realisation of something which is in the nature of a work of art .... It is, in fact, a conception of a metropolis as a centre of life, of civilisation, more intense, more eager, more vitalising than has ever so far been obtained.'

South Harrow, 1935.
The lone passenger
in this photograph
is standing in an
environment created
entirely by London
Transport and its
precursor the
Underground Group.
The new station, in the
characteristic house style
of Charles Holden, has
just been completed.
On the left is an ST type
bus, introduced by the
LGOC in 1930, and a
new concrete bus stop.
The bus crew and station
staff member are wearing
their new London
Transport uniforms.
On the right are
prominently displayed
publicity posters, an
early version of Harry
Beck's diagrammatic
Underground map and a
London Transport bull's-
eye sign with lettering
in Edward Johnston's
Underground typeface.

Introduction

Despite many attempts to demonstrate the
importance of good design both to business
and to society at large, the design process is
still given very little credibility. As everything
that is not organic is in some way designed,
this is both surprising and disappointing –
especially when one considers that in this
century there have been some notable
examples of a successful enterprise
distinguishing itself from its competitors
through a commitment to good design. Sadly,
analysis shows that the successes were usually
built on the vision of one individual whose
belief in the power of design changed a
culture or a business. When that individual
departs, the belief withers and rarely seems to
pass to the next generation.

The history of design in London Transport
partly mirrors this experience. The
organisation's reputation for good design and
architecture was built on the convictions of
one man, Frank Pick, whose energy and vision
changed the face of transport in London,
indeed changed the face of London itself. Pick,
encouraged it must be said by his Chairman
Lord Ashfield, employed some of the best
architects and designers of his day, secure in
the belief that everything must be 'fit for
purpose', and that only the best would suffice.
His success can be measured by the things he
left behind; the buildings, the lettering, the
posters. It was well summarised by the critic
Nikolaus Pevsner, writing in 1942 just after
Pick's death:

> That London Transport stands for an
> architecture unequalled by transport
> design in any other metropolis, and that it
> has by means of its buildings and publicity
> become the most efficacious centre of
> visual education in England, is due to one
> man. Without Frank Pick, London's
> transport system may have developed into
> something no less extensive and well

Visual images that all
say London Transport.
A poster by Trickett
and Webb celebrating
the 60th anniversary
of London Transport's
creation, 1993.

SIXTY YEARS PASSENGER SERVICE FOR THE CAPITAL

working than we know it today (although this is doubtful, too) but it would certainly not be the civilising agent that it is.

That this book is dedicated to Pick is entirely appropriate. On a broader level it is also dedicated to the idea that good, well-managed design can change the culture of a business and the way it is perceived by its customers. We have taken a fairly broad definition of design and looked at it in terms of corporate identity, the visual and functional elements that constitute an organisation's personality. Today many large organisations use design in this way as a means of defining and promoting their character both internally for their members and employees, and externally to customers and the wider world. It is a way for any organisation to say who they are through what they do (products), how they do it (information) and where they do it (environments). In London Transport's case these three elements of corporate identity are represented by vehicles and rolling stock (products), posters and other publicity (information) and architecture/engineering (environments). London Transport and its immediate predecessor the Underground Group were pioneers in the conscious development of a strong and progressive corporate identity long before the term was first coined.

We have used the three elements of corporate identity as a ready-made format for this book. The first section provides an overview of design development in London Transport through corporate identity. This is followed by sections on the three constituent elements of that identity. In each case we start with a brief examination of how design featured (or, in most cases, did not feature) in the operation of London's Victorian public transport companies. We then consider how, in the early twentieth century, mechanisation and amalgamation brought these individual

organisations together into a corporate whole in which design came to play an influential role. Finally, we look at how the corporate vision of London Transport design under Pick has fared in the half century since his departure. The book shows, we hope, that London Transport still retains some of Pick's idealism and beliefs, and that these have been, and will be in the future, of enormous and continuing benefit to the business, its staff, and most importantly, to its passengers.

When writing the book, the question was never what to put in – there is more than enough material – but what to leave out. Certain things are missing; some areas are not covered, some are only mentioned in passing. This is not an official history of London Transport design, nor a comprehensive one. All opinions expressed are our own except where others are quoted. This is our personal view of a remarkable transport system and the buildings, artefacts and images that made it, and still make it, exceptional.

Oliver Green
Jeremy Rewse-Davies

Corporate Identity is at the heart of every business, whether the business recognises it or not. London Transport was fortunate at the outset in having in Frank Pick a Chief Executive who understood that it was as important to communicate the objectives and purposes of the organisation as it was to actually provide the service. For Pick, good design was good business, but equally important

Left: Instantly recognisable symbols of London Transport – the roundel and the red double-decker bus.

was his understanding that design was a business tool that could, amongst other things, communicate

Below: An early Underground promotional sticker using the bull's-eye symbol, about 1910.

to passengers what sort of business London

Opposite: London Transport Corporate Identity Guidelines, 1991.

Transport was; and to staff what sort of business he intended it to be. Pick was not alone in having this awareness of what design could do, but his innate understanding of what is now called corporate identity was ahead of its time. Even today very few companies communicate their purpose as clearly as London Transport did in the 1930s.

Below, left to right:
The development of the
London Transport symbol.
Underground Group
publicity device, 1907;
LGOC winged wheel cap
badge, 1910; Underground
station 'bull's-eye'
nameboard, c1908;
London Transport bar
and circle, 1933; London
Transport Trolleybus
symbol, c1935; London
Transport roundel, 1972.

There are many different
stories about the design
and development of the
'roundel', including one
well-authenticated
account in which Frank
Pick is reported to have
said that it was a copy of
the Plimsoll line device.
An interesting version
is that it developed
from a visit to Paris in
1907 by Albert Stanley
(later Lord Ashfield).

The Birth of a Corporate Style

During the early years of the twentieth century a number of companies providing public transport in London amalgamated into the larger, privately owned Underground Group, which in turn purchased other tram and bus companies to complement its subway services. The Group established a form of visual focus for itself through the use of a logo which incorporated a tram-car, underground railway lines and symbols of electrical power. The Group also developed a limited architectural vocabulary with its platforms and stations for the new tube lines, opened in 1906–7. Three lines were opened, all run by separate subsidiaries, and all with the same station design. A consistent Underground lettering style was used outside every station. The present London Transport bull's-eye device or 'roundel' evolved gradually from the imagery used by the Underground Group, early examples of which can still be seen on platform nameplates at Caledonian Road and Arsenal stations.

In 1915 Pick asked Edward Johnston, a leading calligrapher, to develop a letter face to be used for station signage and posters (see page 81). Johnston worked with the Underground Group and then London Transport for the rest of his life, providing numerous variations of the typeface he had first developed in 1916. This typeface, 'The Underground Railway Block' letter alphabet, has been one of the most influential pieces of work on type this century and is the font from which all modern sans serif faces have been developed. The updated and redrawn version 'New Johnston' is still in use today (see page 83).

The Johnston typeface and the roundel have been the basis of the identity of the Underground Group and then London Transport for the greater part of this century. After the creation of London Transport in 1933 with its broad responsibilities for the movement of people in the capital, Pick used these two main facets of the identity to unite visually the whole group. With a single public authority responsible for all bus, tram and

He noticed that the names of the stations on the Paris Metro were shown in small-size type displayed in a clear space approximately 12ft. high x 6ft. wide and situated at even intervals along

the length of each platform.
Stanley thought that this would be an improvement on the method of naming stations then current in London, which consisted

of three large name boards, one at each end and one in the middle of the platform. It was decided to try out new Paris Metro-style signs at St James's Park station and to erect boards 12ft.

x 6ft. with a nameplate 5ft. long. During the period of reconstruction Mr W. Cleal, the Station Inspector of St James's Park, suggested to Stanley that the station's name should be distinguished

in some way from all the other advertisements appearing on the platforms. This suggestion gave Stanley the idea of creating a symbol that would act as a 'trade mark' for the

underground railway operations in London, it was possible, indeed necessary, to develop a design ethic for the whole organisation. Pick saw the possibilities for using design as a means of 'harnessing commercial methods to the achievement of large social objectives'.

There were other reasons for London Transport's interest in its corporate style. The new single body incorporated over ninety independent bus companies and municipal tramways as well as the large Underground Group. Not all the companies were keen to become part of the group, and loyalty to some of the smaller, privately owned ones was strong. The new Board saw immediately that if the group was to function effectively it must replace that loyalty with an allegiance to the new organisation. It set out to foster that allegiance in two ways: first, by harmonising all wages, working conditions and operating rules, and second, by the creation of a strong corporate style that encompassed every aspect of London Transport's activities. The new identity was used as an effective business tool

to unite the workforce, and was immediately apparent on liveries, uniforms, signage and printed material.

The remarkable thing about this early exercise in corporate identity is not that it existed at all, but that it was so sophisticated and stylish. Not for Pick the monoculture of the carefully controlled image, the proscriptive rules, the 'single voice'. The

Above: The early Underground lettering style and bull's-eye could be used for jokey promotions as well as serious corporate identity, as in this cartoon by Charles Pears from his *Alphabet for T.O.T*, published by the Underground in 1914.

Underground Group and at the same time draw attention to the station nameplate. After further consultation Stanley finally selected a red disc with the station name printed across it in a bar.

The 'bull's-eye' was soon adopted as the standard symbol for all Underground station names.

Towards the end of the First World War, Frank Pick pointed out that the

bull's-eye sign was spoilt by the fact that there was nothing in it to hold the eye. After making many sketches, Pick found that by changing the disc into a ring the eye was not only attracted but also

held by the white centre. He then asked Edward Johnston, the typographer, to prepare a symbol of this type, making the proportions between the bar and the circle as attractive to the

eye as possible. The Johnston design was registered to prevent others copying it (Reg. No. 659814).

images that emerged were witty and cultured, and promoted the idea of a progressive, efficient, caring and style-conscious organisation. This was done through the use of the best graphic designers, illustrators and typographers, and on a different level through the architecture and vehicles. All the designers involved were allowed to work in their own way provided the result said in broad terms what Pick wanted. The results were varied and often brilliant but used corporate images in what today could be an unacceptably cavalier manner.

In other areas the visual imagery was just as apparently cavalier – station roundels, bus stops, shelters, even the buildings displaying an amazing diversity and yet having a unity of message about the organisation that is probably unique. Pick did not even appear to worry about the use of typefaces, provided that Johnston was used for station signage and important communications. In other areas Gill, Johnston and Times Roman were all used freely. Pick understood the importance of

differing tones of voice for different messages, as the astonishing range of the advertising and publicity material of his day shows.

As with other parts of this great transport enterprise, corporate identity and communications were based on the pursuit of excellence and fitness for purpose: pursuit of excellence through the use of the most creative talent of the day and fitness for purpose through the application of simple design principles to everything, from a component produced for a train or bus down to the smallest press advertisement. Pick's philosophy is best summed up in his own words: 'The test of the goodness of a thing is its fitness for use. If it fails on this first test, no amount of ornamentation or finish will make it any better; it will only make it more expensive, more foolish.'

The use of good design became a tradition but was never 'traditional'. The main characteristics were a willingness to seek new ideas and solutions, to experiment with new methods and materials, unrestricted by the

Right: An early exercise in testing the application of corporate identity to station façades, with the lettering hand-painted on to a photograph of Edgware Road station. The distinctive UNDERGROUND lettering with a larger first and last letter, was adopted as the corporate style for all the Underground Group's railways in 1908.

UNDERGROUND

GETS YOU THERE

-KEEPS LONDON GOING

Above: Trainee bus conductors, 1935. Corporate identity used effectively to unite staff under one 'flag'. This is the standard London Transport Central Buses navy-blue uniform worn with a white summer cap cover.

Far left: Poster by Zéro (Hans Schleger), 1935. Schleger used the artful watch/roundel image more than once. Here the symbol also appears as a passenger's spectacles.

Left: Poster by Man Ray, 1939. A brilliant adaptation of the corporate symbol, taking London Transport into another world.

past. Through proper management of design, London Transport was able to present a consolidated and unified message to the travelling public that every care had been taken in providing them with the best possible service that was safe, easy and convenient to use.

Inevitably this state of affairs did not last. After the war London Transport had a new Chairman and a new constitution from 1948 as the London Transport Executive, one of the five parts of the nationalised British Transport Commission which controlled all aspects of public transport except air traffic. What they did not have was a replacement for Frank Pick who had died in 1941, and although the programme of works continued, the creative force was missing. It was not that London Transport changed creative direction; rather the direction faltered and finally disappeared. For some years after the war, the enterprise

that Pick and his Chairman Lord Ashfield had built remained visually intact, albeit with the scars of war showing in many places. Some of the spirit of Pick lived on, either in buildings that had been designed before the war and completed afterwards, such as Gants Hill, or in new stations such as White City (1947), which still shows a simplicity and clarity that would not have been out of place ten or fifteen years before. Communications also showed that the purposes of the business were still well understood by its directors and managers; artists such as Tom Eckersley, Hans Unger and Abram Games were still producing distinguished and effective posters. Photographs of the system right up until the very late 1950s reveal how little had changed since the 1930s. However, in the next twenty-five years almost every aspect of the system was to change beyond recognition.

Loss of Direction

Until the war the corporate identity and design management of the system was under the control of one man. There was therefore no perceived need to set up any supporting management structure. After the war, with that one man sadly gone, the management of design fell increasingly to department heads such as the Chief Architect, the Chief Mechanical Engineer and the Publicity Officer. Inevitably in this type of situation, where direction comes from more than one source, the result lacks cohesion. During the 1950s and early 1960s, although some good work was done, notably with the Routemaster bus, there was little feeling of unity about the various elements, no 'corporate feel'.

In 1963, realising perhaps that there was, if not a creative vacuum, then at least a lack of coherence, London Transport set up a Design Committee for the first time and included on it a design consultant, Misha Black. Black was in some ways as interesting and inspirational as Pick, although with a smaller canvas. He had been responsible with Milner Gray for setting up Design Research Unit, one of the first British design consultancies, and in 1933 had been part of the group that founded the Society of Industrial Artists, now the Chartered Society of Designers. It is interesting that forty years after Pick, Black wrote an article called 'Fitness for Purpose'; what he said could have been said by Pick:

> We should approach each new problem from the base of practicality – how can it most economically be made, how will it function most effectively, how can maintenance be simplified, how can the use of scarce materials be minimised? An absolute concern with practicalities will produce new formal solutions as technology constantly develops: when alternatives present themselves during the design process, the aesthetic sensitivity of

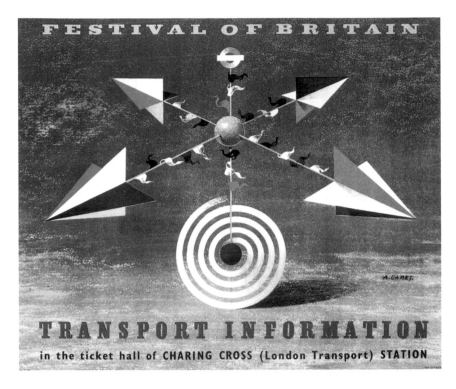

the designer will determine his selective decision but this should remain a searching process and not be seen as the opportunity for imposing a preconception of formal appropriateness. The difference between an arrogant conscious aesthetic and a conscientious searching for the most elegant solution is fundamental to my argument.

The influence of Black on the panel can be seen most clearly in the Victoria Line for which he was also design consultant. There appears to be an attempt to return to the simple forms of the 1930s and to co-ordinate once again every aspect of the corporate voice. The trains, stations, hardware and posters for the Victoria Line had a similarity of expression that announced that London Transport was once again concerned with its identity, and with the way it presented itself.

However, looking back it can be seen that the brief period of Misha Black's involvement was ultimately to have little lasting influence (the Victoria Line was criticised for being dull and drab), and the concept of a co-ordinated

Above: Festival of Britain poster by Abram Games, 1951.

Right: Tom Eckersley's dramatic poster for the opening of the Victoria Line in 1969.

Far right: The Victoria Line projected a strong sixties image with its simple shapes and unpainted trains, implying high efficiency through the use of advanced technology. The image was rather diluted by the cost-cutting measures that reduced the specification of some of the materials, such as the tiling, to no more than domestic quality.

house style or corporate identity receded. It was a reflection of the times that London Transport's design policy during the 1970s and early 1980s turned to individual expression and to decoration rather than fitness for purpose. This was partly caused by the need to attract people on to the system; for some years passenger traffic on the Underground had declined, and the response was to try and enliven the stations and the travelling experience by the use of decoration. This policy, whilst attracting a great deal of attention and critical acclaim from the travelling public, was not well enough articulated and carried through to give a cohesive feel to the system. It was if anything nearer in spirit to the entertainment industry, and is best summed up as 'good in parts'.

New Beginnings

In 1984, with London Transport emerging in yet another guise as London Regional Transport, an attempt was made to separate the planning and organising body from the operating subsidiaries in order that they could be managed as separate entities. It was decided to explain this change by the introduction of a new symbol for LRT, as it became known.

Above: London Regional Transport was created in 1984 with a new symbol for the Corporate Centre, visually separated from the operating side of the business, but the LRT name and symbol were soon abandoned.

Right: London Buses subsidiary company logo, 1980s.

The operating subsidiaries were each set up as limited companies and had their own version of the roundel. London Underground Limited had a blue bar and London Buses Limited a yellow bar. The red roundel was left to signify multimodal services such as travelcards, and infrastructure such as bus stops. The idea was to give a separate visual style to each of the subsidiaries and yet link them to the transport family of operating companies. The LRT symbol was self-effacing to denote a 'hands-off' planning and organising body with no direct responsibility for day-to-day operations.

The result was not well understood by the public and was unpopular with staff. However, the Fennel Report in 1988 on the King's Cross fire disaster made it clear that London Transport could not take a hands-off position with its subsidiaries, and the new Chairman Wilfrid Newton moved swiftly to reinstate the plain red roundel as London Transport's symbol, linking it firmly to the operational side of the business. At the same time the description 'London Regional Transport' was dropped for all but legal uses and LRT reverted to being London Transport.

At the time of the creation of London Regional Transport there was an assumption that the bus companies, along with some non-core businesses, would be privatised in the foreseeable future. As a first step towards this, London Buses Limited created five separate districts with their own logos; within two or three years these had become ten subsidiary companies, each with their own company name and logo. Although these names and symbols applied to the buses meant very little to the travelling public, they were important to the workforce as a focus for the new companies and were intended to engender loyalty. This of course is exactly the reverse of the process that took place in 1933, but the methods were identical. It is perhaps unfortunate that the images used were poor and in some cases inappropriate. The smaller transport-related companies developed a number of identities usually based on the roundel or a derivation of it, but again most of the images were uninspiring and lacked style and conviction.

The return to the red roundel for London Transport in 1989 was an opportunity to try to bring all the central group of companies back under one umbrella and to give some visual coherence to the group. At the same time strenuous efforts were being made to tackle the other aspects of the group's identity – environments and products. Clearly

Above: Buses in every colour have appeared in London since route tendering began in the late 1980s. The buses shown here are owned by various private companies that now operate routes on London Transport's behalf.

Left: London Underground Limited Vehicle Livery manual: clear, simple and well presented.

Far left: The LT Pass Agent business was one of many in the late 1980s allowed to develop their own secondary marks to help explain the business to their customers. The roundel is used as an official endorsement.

there was a need to return to Pick's dictum of fitness for purpose, and to try to promote the business identity through design excellence. The need to explain the organisation, and what it was about, to the travelling public was even greater. The political agenda included not only the disposal of the London bus companies but also the tendering of an increasing percentage of routes. This resulted in a patchwork of differently coloured buses

London Transport's corporate identity is also part of London's identity. Paul Hogarth's drawing of Piccadilly Circus shows the contribution that London Transport's symbols and artefacts have made to the visitor's idea of London.

plying their trade in central London – a situation which the public did not understand. Some of the non-core businesses were closed and others were to be privatised. The resultant changing scene both inside and outside the business prompted the need for an identity that was simple, based on the roundel and the Johnston typeface as core elements, yet with the flexibility to encompass almost continual change for the foreseeable future.

Design Management took the decision to give the central departments and the trading group the type of leeway that Pick had allowed in the 1930s. Each small trading unit was given a secondary 'marketing' identity to be used in conjunction with the roundel. A second typeface, Bembo, was introduced to be used with New Johnston, and some very basic rules were drawn up to guide the users. There was training of managers in the use and management of design, and a great deal of encouragement to be creative, and to use the best designers wherever possible.

That the constituent parts of the organisation were becoming more independent is evident in the rather different view of communication policy taken by the Underground and London Buses, who preferred to use New Johnston for all purposes. There was, however, a consensus about the approach needed for environments and hardware; both were to be designed in a way that projected the message as simply and clearly as possible. The first manifestation of this new approach to identity and communication were in-house manuals, notably *How to Use the London Transport Corporate Identity*, which set out the policy and how it was to be implemented, and *Simple Rules* – four very slim manuals which contained the basic 'do's and don'ts' of using the identity.

Other examples of the return to simplicity and clarity and to 'fitness for purpose' began to manifest themselves throughout the system.

New products and signage, new bus stops and bus information, new station designs at Angel and Hammersmith and the projected designs of both the Jubilee Line extension and CrossRail, show the same commitment to excellence and innovation and to a corporate vision. Through its present design policies London Transport is again using design in the way that Pick did sixty years ago, to communicate the purposes of the company to passengers and staff and to play a major part in promoting to the public the image of a safe, progressive, efficient and well-managed enterprise.

Vehicles and rolling stock designed to the highest technical standards are crucial to any public transport organisation if it is to provide a reliable service. The vehicles also need to attract customers in the first place and be capable of carrying large numbers of people in reasonable comfort. Good vehicle design is therefore a combination of technical efficiency, ergonomics and practical aesthetics, qualities which London Transport, in its heyday, came to epitomise. For

Below: 1973 stock, the development of the classic tube train body profile perfected in the 1930s.

Bottom: Symbol of a long partnership. An AEC blue triangle bus radiator badge incorporating the London Transport roundel.

most of the nineteenth century, public transport in London relied on horse and steam power for locomotion. The electric motor and the petrol engine transformed London's buses, trams and underground trains in the 1900s, creating a transport revolution within a decade. Vehicles which had not changed substantially in design for more than thirty years emerged in mechanised form larger, faster and more comfortable for passengers.

Left: The epitome of high-quality London Transport vehicle design. This is the prototype Routemaster RM1, built in 1954, photographed in 1956 on its first day of passenger service.

The Victorian Inheritance

In the second half of the nineteenth century horse-bus operations in the capital were dominated by the London General Omnibus (named after the Victorian domestic knife cleaning board it resembled) was replaced by forward-facing slatted 'garden' seating. The construction and maintenance of the LGOC's

Above right: LGOC horse buses outside the Crown Hotel, Cricklewood in about 1902. On the right a crowd has gathered to look at the future – a new motor bus.

Right: One of the first successful horse trams, introduced in 1870. With twice the loading capacity of horse buses, trams could operate profitably on much lower fares and quickly became the first method of transport that a majority of Londoners could afford to use regularly.

Company. Soon after its creation in 1856, the LGOC developed a more or less standard design of vehicle which met its basic requirements, but then did little to improve it. Operating experience had shown that in the crowded streets of London a sturdy, compact and manoeuvrable bus which could be handled comfortably by two horses was ideal. These practical considerations determined the maximum width and weight of the vehicle. A standard London horse bus had room inside for about twelve passengers, with outside seating on the roof and beside the driver for another twelve. In fifty years the only significant changes to this standard layout were the addition of a curved staircase at the back of the bus instead of the precarious original iron rungs giving access to the upper deck, and a new seating arrangement on the roof. The single, back-to-back 'knifeboard' seat

extensive fleet was a labour-intensive craft operation which the company carried out in its own workshops.

The only rival mass transit system on the streets of London was provided by the horse tramways, which began operation in the 1870s. Two horses could manage a much larger vehicle if it was running on smooth metal rails instead of an uneven road surface.

A horse tram could weigh a couple of tonnes and seat up to fifty passengers – about twice the weight and capacity of an omnibus. The design of the vehicles was very similar to that of omnibuses except that tramcars were double ended and could be driven in both directions. At the terminus the horses were unhitched and taken to the opposite end of the tram to be re-attached for the return journey. The tram itself was not turned round, but the seat backs were reversed to face the direction of the travel.

Early tramcars were supplied to the operating companies by established coach builders, some even being imported from the USA, where the first tramway systems had opened. As the companies grew, however, they developed the facilities to build and repair their own vehicles. Like omnibuses, tramcars were largely of traditional wooden construction, hand-built to a very high standard in order to survive their daily battering from hundreds of travellers. It is no exaggeration to suggest that London's first

really cheap public transport system used vehicles designed to a specification which was superior to any private carriage of the time.

The first two underground railways in London, the Metropolitan and the District, both began operations in the 1860s. The trains were much like the rolling stock used by main-line railways except that they were hauled by steam locomotives fitted with special condensing apparatus to reduce steam and smoke emission in the tunnels. This was the only design concession to underground operation and it was not very effective at easing the fundamental problem of ventilation. Passengers travelled in carriages of similar design to the 'overground' suburban lines. The short, wooden coach bodies were divided into compartments ranging in comfort from 1st to 3rd class, each with front-and-back facing seats and slam doors. It was hardly surprising that the steam underground, with its sulphurous subterranean environment of dirt and smoke, had a rather poor public image.

Left: District Railway steam train at West Brompton, 1876. The large pipe on the side of the locomotive is the condensing apparatus, a rather crude and ineffectual method of reducing steam emission in the tunnels.

Above: New LGOC
B type buses about to
enter service from
Cricklewood Garage,
1911, with the crews
wearing their smart new
uniforms.

Motor Buses

The main expense in horse-bus operation was feeding and caring for the animals. This encouraged the search for an alternative form of motive power. The first regular service in London using petrol-engined motor buses, introduced in 1899, lasted for just over a year. More reliable engines were developed, and in 1905 the first boom in motor-bus operation took place, with a series of small independent companies entering the field. Three years later the LGOC, which still ran the largest horse-bus fleet, made a successful takeover bid for its two principal rivals in motor-bus operation. The combined expertise of all three companies was then pooled to develop a standard design. This eventually emerged in October 1910 as the famous B type.

The B type was designed by Frank Searle, the LGOC's Chief Engineer, who cheerfully

acknowledged having 'cribbed shamelessly' in its development. As he said of the X type, the immediate predecessor of the B type, 'any parts of the 28 types which had stood up to the gruelling of the London streets were embodied in it'. Hybrid it may have been, but the B type was a winning combination of parts. To produce its new bus the LGOC decided to set up a fully equipped manufacturing plant in Walthamstow. Nearly 3,000 B type engine units and chassis were turned out here at the rate of 20 per week, a quantity and speed then unrivalled by any motor manufacturer in Britain. Unfortunately this impressive move to mass-production methods could not yet be matched on the wooden body-building side, which carried on in traditional craft style at the LGOC's three coach works.

Despite mechanisation, the overall layout and design of buses still reflected that of their horse-drawn predecessors. Even where advances became technically possible, progress was often held back by the stringent licensing regulations imposed in London by the Metropolitan Police. These included strict limits on weight, length, width and seating capacity. Primitive though it looked, the open-top 34-seat B type was probably the best that could have been achieved within these regulations in 1910.

The new buses were so successful in service that within a year of their introduction the LGOC was able to replace all its remaining horse buses. In 1912 the newly mechanised LGOC was absorbed by the Underground Group. Instead of competing with the Underground, the bus network, already growing fast, was now developed as a feeder system to it, and the outer Underground termini became the starting points for new Sunday bus services running out into London's countryside. There was also a strengthening of the hesitant early moves towards establishing a visual identity for the company. Horse-bus

routes had often been worked by associations of different operators, and the colour of a bus indicated its route rather than its ownership. In 1908 the LGOC introduced route numbers and chose the now familiar bright red as the standard colour for all its motor buses. The name General had already begun to appear in large letters on the sides of buses, together with the first LGOC logo, a winged wheel device. This design also appeared on cap badges as part of the staff uniforms first issued by the LGOC to its bus crews in 1910.

After the Underground Group takeover, the LGOC's Walthamstow works was set up as a separate bus-manufacturing subsidiary, the Associated Equipment Company. AEC, which moved in the 1920s to a new west London site at Southall, was to remain the principal supplier of London's buses for over fifty years. Throughout this period there was a close relationship between operator and supplier which enabled bus design to be developed jointly to the particular requirements of first the LGOC and, after

Below left: A B type in Charles Pears' children's alphabet of 1914. As well as being ubiquitous in London, these buses were soon being used as troop carriers on the Western Front for the duration of the First World War.

Below: AEC maker's plate and LGOC radiator badge from a K type bus, the successor to the B type introduced in 1919.

B is the useful ubiquitous Bus,
A good way to travel for you and for us.

Right: A traffic scene at Marble Arch in 1930 showing how dramatically bus design had developed in the 1920s. The solid-tyred, open-top K type of 1919 (centre) was succeeded by the pneumatic-tyred and covered-top version of the NS type from 1925 (left and far right) and finally the new, fully enclosed ST type (right).

Below right: Even behind the scenes activities were carefully publicised. This glossy brochure on Chiswick Works with a cover design by E. McKnight Kauffer was published in 1932.

1933, London Transport. AEC became a fully independent company in 1933, but London Transport contracted to buy most of its chassis and spares from them for the next ten years. AEC's dominance of the London bus market continued until its takeover by Leyland in the 1960s.

The LGOC opened its own centralised bus overhaul and maintenance works at Chiswick in 1921. Every vehicle in the fleet was sent to Chiswick once a year to be completely stripped down and virtually rebuilt. The workshops also built bodies for new chassis, although by the 1930s there was an increasing tendency to use external body builders working to Chiswick's specifications. When London Transport took over in 1933, Chiswick was already carrying out its own rigorous testing and experimental work before making any major changes in the company's bus engineering and design. London Transport built on Chiswick's reputation for setting design standards in the bus industry and, because of its size and influence, was able

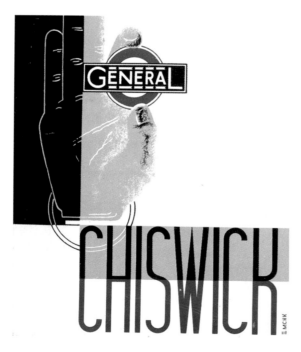

to ensure that its suppliers met them. Eventually, from the 1960s onwards, this long-held dominance began a continuous

downward slide. By the 1990s Chiswick had closed and London Transport's bus engineering role had disappeared completely.

During the 1920s buses lost nearly all traces of their horse-drawn ancestry and began to resemble modern vehicles. It was a decade of particularly dramatic design development, aided by the gradual relaxation of the licensing regulations. Seating capacity increased as the size of vehicles grew, enclosed top decks were allowed, pneumatic tyres replaced solid rubber, roller blinds were introduced instead of wooden destination boards and fully upholstered seats became a standard feature.

Many of the improvements were stimulated by competition between the LGOC and a rash of new independent bus operators, dismissively branded as 'pirates' by the General. The independents were mostly

decker and Renown six-wheel double decker. Production models of all three, classified by the LGOC as T, ST and LT types, were on the streets of London by 1930.

After 1933 London Transport followed the LGOC's policy of standardising its bus fleet as far as possible. Double deckers remained the standard high-capacity London vehicles with some single deckers for hilly or lightly used suburban and country routes. Single-deck coaches were also required for excursion services and for use on the new Green Line routes introduced from 1930 onwards, which ran out to towns in London's countryside. At its very first meeting in July 1933 the new Board took the important decision to use oil (diesel) engines in all its buses, on the basis that this would save some £120 a year in the running costs of each vehicle. With this move, which followed extensive experimental trials by the LGOC, London Transport set a national trend. All subsequent new orders were for diesel buses, although because of the war, conversion of the existing petrol-engined

Below: Newly delivered 10T10 Green Line coaches ready for service at Hemel Hempstead Garage, 1938. These vehicles had AEC Regal chassis with diesel engines and bodywork designed and built by London Transport at Chiswick.

supplied by rival manufacturers to AEC, such as Dennis and Leyland. It was Leyland's Chief Engineer John Rackham who designed the Titan in 1927, a real breakthrough in bus design and a considerable improvement on the latest AEC/LGOC vehicle, the NS type of 1923. The Titan boasted a six-cylinder overhead camshaft engine to the NS type's four-cylinder side valve unit. It also had a chassis layout which enabled a low-slung body to be fitted, and this in turn was designed to take lightweight aluminium panelling throughout. In short, the Leyland Titan was the first modern bus.

Within a year of the Titan's appearance, Rackham had been head-hunted by AEC with the brief to create a new range of buses which could compete effectively with his own new Leylands. The result was the AEC Regal single decker, Regent four-wheel double

fleet was not completed until 1950.

The standard London Transport bus of the 1930s was the STL type, which used a lengthened version of the AEC Regent chassis. Its body layout, essentially a fully enclosed box except for the half cab and open rear platform, remained the archetypal form of the London

ARRANGEMENT OF 56 SEATER DOUBLE DECK BUS (Central)
Approved Colour Scheme.

Above right: Approved
colour scheme for an
STL type bus, from a
hand-painted
specification book
prepared at Chiswick
Works in the late 1940s.

Transport double-decker bus until the 1960s.
The design was a functional but rather
conservative solution to the basic question of
what a bus should be like, and it certainly did
not match up to the sleek modernity of
contemporary Underground trains and
stations. Frank Pick clearly hoped that bus
design could be improved to the standards
of the rail business, but he was to be
disappointed. When he went on an
architectural study tour of Northern Europe
with his consultant architect Charles Holden
in 1930, Pick was particularly impressed with
the new buses and trams they saw in
Copenhagen, which had been designed by
the city architect. On their return, Pick asked
Holden to devise a better bus design for
London, but the surviving drawings from
Holden's office show no significant change or
improvement from the then current LGOC

vehicles. Whatever his skills as an architect,
Holden was no industrial designer. His bus
stayed on the drawing board and the radical
ideas in vehicle development in the 1930s
came not from an architect but from the
engineers and draughtsmen at Chiswick
working with the manufacturers.

Many of the experiments tried out in this
period now seem to have been ahead of their
time and were only taken up many years later.
The AEC Q type of 1932, for example, had a
side-mounted engine which allowed a front-
entrance double-deck body to be fitted. It
looks very similar to the design style adopted
almost universally for British double deckers
since the 1960s, but it was not a success in its
day. Later experiments with an underfloor
engine gave even more scope for changing the
body design and layout. This was first tried
out in 1939 with the elegant TF type coach,

Left: The AEC Q type chassis had a side-mounted engine which allowed a front-entrance body to be fitted. Q2 was the first of four double-deck prototypes introduced in 1934. It was only mass produced in a single-deck version.

Below left: The sleek curved lines of the TF type Green Line coach introduced in 1939 concealed a horizontally mounted underfloor engine. Notice the London Transport bar and circle device framing the radiator cap.

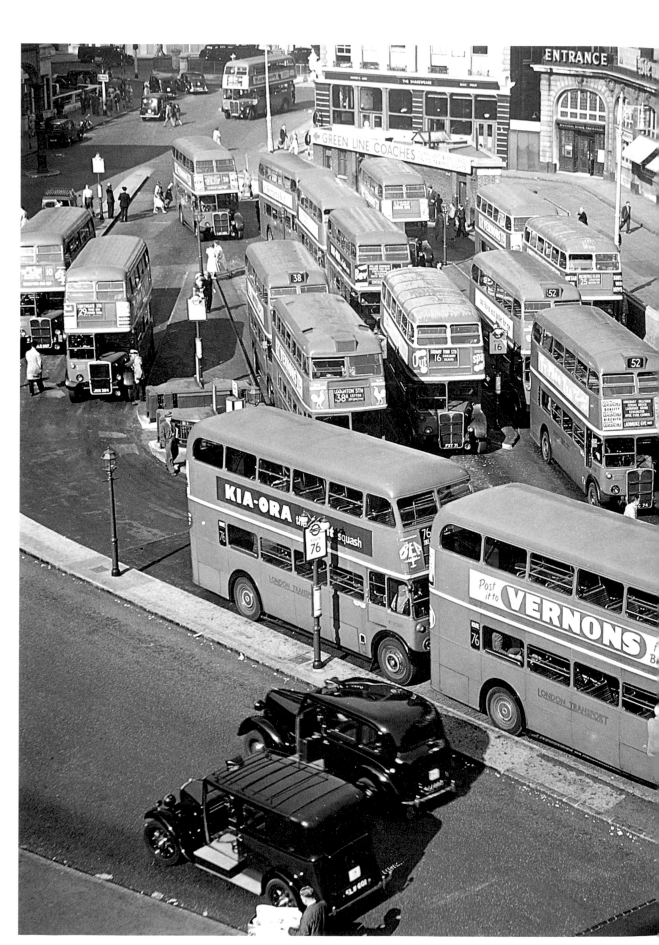

Standardising the fleet. All but one of the 18 buses seen here at Victoria bus station in 1953 is from the post-war RT family.

built on a Leyland Tiger chassis, which foreshadowed many post-war developments.

For the majority of its fleet, London Transport followed an evolutionary rather than a revolutionary design development process. This was certainly true of the classic RT (Regent Three) type, which was eventually mass-produced in greater quantity than any other bus. When the prototype appeared in 1939 it did not look very different to the STL, but in every detail its design conformed to the high-quality, practical and by this stage rather refined and elegant Chiswick approach. Not surprisingly, Eric Ottaway, who was London Transport's Technical Officer (Buses and Coaches) and led the design and engineering team at Chiswick, had also worked for AEC at Southall before 1933.

Mass production of the RT did not start until the late 1940s when valuable lessons in the standardisation of components learned while London Transport built Halifax bomber aircraft during the war were incorporated in the post-war design. Nearly 7,000 buses of the RT family were completed by two chassis builders (AEC and Leyland) and six body builders to give London Transport the world's largest standardised bus fleet in the mid-1950s. An even bigger overhaul works was opened at Aldenham, on the edge of north London, where the enormous scale of London Transport's bus operations could best be appreciated: 1,800 staff were employed to turn out more than fifty completely overhauled buses every week. In fact by the time Aldenham became fully operational in 1956, what had seemed in the 1940s to be an ever-expanding demand for bus services in London was already dropping, and London Transport soon found itself with too many vehicles and under-used facilities. The central overhaul facilities were eventually wound down in the 1980s, and Aldenham was closed in 1987.

Overleaf: RT type buses inside London Transport's massive bus overhaul works at Aldenham, fully commissioned in 1956 but closed just over thirty years later when a central overhaul system was abandoned as too costly.

Designing the Routemaster

London Transport's well-established tradition of excellence in bus engineering and design is epitomised by the Routemaster, first developed in the early 1950s and likely to be seen on the streets of London beyond the year 2000. It represents London Transport bus design at its peak, the product of a long and

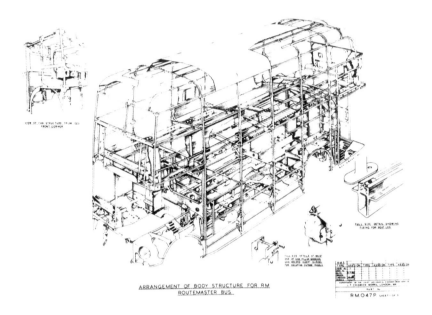

ARRANGEMENT OF BODY STRUCTURE FOR RM
ROUTEMASTER BUS

R.M.O.47.P

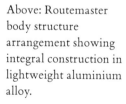

Above: Routemaster body structure arrangement showing integral construction in lightweight aluminium alloy.

exhaustive development programme with extensive trials of four very different prototypes over a five-year period before production of a standard model began. Despite the proven quality and long life of the final design, expensive research and development on this scale to perfect a bus specially for London is unlikely ever to happen again.

The Routemaster project developed out of London Transport's need for a new diesel bus large enough to replace its 70-seat trolleybuses on a one-for-one basis. When buses were used to replace the remaining trams in 1950–52, 56-seat RTs took over from 77-seat trams, and more buses than trams were consequently needed to maintain loading capacity. The challenge was to design a new bus which was within the statutory dimensions then current (a maximum length of 27ft. 6in. and width of

8ft.) and was no heavier than the RT type, but which could carry more passengers.

The solution lay in the use of lightweight aluminium alloy construction throughout, which made it possible to build a 64-seat bus without increasing the overall weight of the vehicle. Integral construction was used, so there was no separate chassis. The Routemaster has a metal-frame body with a 'stressed skin' which does not require a chassis to give it structural strength. Assembly involves simply bolting the body to separate front and rear running units instead of a chassis. The whole vehicle was designed for close precision mass production using jigs to turn out identical parts. These had to have the maximum possible interchangeability to speed up the overhaul and maintenance process. RM1 was built in 1954 and rigorously tested for two years before entering passenger

Left: A standard 64-seat Routemaster in the livery adopted in the 1970s, when the plain white roundel replaced the gold London Transport fleet lettering used since 1934. The 'Pirelli Slippers' advertisement was one of the earliest creative uses of bus side advertising by Fletcher Forbes Gill in 1963.

Below: Production model Routemaster newly delivered from manufacturers AEC and Park Royal Vehicles, 1961. The Guinness advertisement on the side is by Tom Eckersley, who also designed numerous publicity posters for London Transport over five decades.

service in 1956. Three other Routemaster prototypes, each one an experiment with different features, followed in 1957, with production models finally available for service from 1959.

The design process on the Routemaster was preceded by a comprehensive review of all operating requirements in order to establish the form which the new vehicle should take. Bill Durrant, who had been London Transport's Chief Mechanical Engineer (Road Services) since 1933, and was very much the inspiration behind the Routemaster project, later described the first stage: 'We asked the Operating Managers to try to erase from their minds all past features they had specified, to think out their requirements from rock bottom ... the aim being to get down to the ideal bus from their point of view.' At a time when private car

ownership was beginning to rise dramatically and to compete with bus travel, it was also important to improve bus design and comfort from the passenger's point of view. The Routemaster was therefore given independent front suspension and coil springs with shock absorbers, already standard features on cars but an innovation for buses which had traditional leaf springs. This gave the Routemaster a ride quality equivalent to that of most saloon cars in the 1960s. The RM was the first London bus to be

Below: Routemaster lower deck interior styled by Douglas Scott. This was essentially a refined version of the pre-war interior design of the RT type developed by London Transport's team at Chiswick.

Above: Green Line coach version of the RF type single decker with body styling by Douglas Scott, 1951.

fitted with a warm air heating system for passenger comfort. It also had power-assisted steering and an automatic gearbox, further contributions to smooth riding which made the Routemaster an easier bus to drive.

The Routemaster was very much a team product and its design should not be attributed to any one individual. Alongside the engineers and draughtsmen at Chiswick working under Durrant and Ottaway (now designated Chief Supplies Officer) were the development staff at AEC and Park Royal Vehicles, the body builders. An external consultant, the industrial designer Douglas Scott, was brought in to work with the London Transport team on the body styling

of the new bus. Scott's involvement followed his successful work on the RF type single decker, which first appeared in both bus and coach variants in 1951. He was largely responsible for the final look of the RF, though his work both on the single decker and later on the Routemaster was a refinement of London Transport's design traditions rather than a break with them. Scott continued the move towards softening the inevitable box-like shape of a bus with radiused curves on all corner surfaces – windows, roof and wheel arches – combined with a strong horizontal emphasis so that the vehicles looked longer rather than bulky or tall. Like the RT, the RF had tubular metal seat frames and grab rails, moquette-covered seating and a subtle combination of interior paintwork and fabric colours. Scott took a similar approach with the Routemaster and was responsible for the restrained tartan moquette seating and interior colour scheme, exotically described as 'Burgundy lining panels, Chinese green window surrounds and Sung yellow ceilings'.

Scott found it more difficult to devise a suitable exterior design for the Routemaster which would be an improvement on the appearance of the RT. London Transport insisted on retaining the half-cab layout because it gives drivers good visibility and prevents passengers from distracting them. As there was no intention at this stage of introducing driver-only operation, the rear open platform remained unchanged and styling development was concentrated on the lower front end of the bus. This went through several design variations on the prototypes before a final style was selected for the production models. The tradition of the large exposed vertical radiator last seen on the RT was now superseded by a much smaller radiator behind a grille set in a lightweight moulded fibreglass surround. Overall, the rounded contours throughout the body design help visually to reduce the bulk of the vehicle and make a large red bus look user-friendly and rather stylish.

The Routemaster was to be the last bus designed for London. By 1968, when a final total of 2,760 Routemasters had been built, London Transport could no longer afford a lengthy research and development programme for its next generation of buses. The Greater London Council, which assumed financial control of London Transport in 1970, followed government inducements (in the form of special bus grants) to buy manufacturers' standard models instead. All new London buses since the late 1960s have been suitable for driver-only operation, having a front-entrance so that passengers can pay the driver as they get on and, usually, a rear-mounted engine. The unique experimental front-entrance rear-engine version of the Routemaster built in 1966 suggests that London Transport would have followed these design trends itself had it been allowed to do so, but with a better quality product. The FRM (front-entrance Routemaster) did not go into production, although ironically the traditional crew-operated RM has outlived many of the 'off the peg' designs bought by London Transport to replace it over the last twenty-five years. The remaining Routemasters, now used only on central London routes, were fitted with new engines and given a full interior refurbishment in the early 1990s to further increase their life expectancy. Old age and nostalgia has endowed the Routemaster with a virtual cult status. It remains exceptionally reliable, functional, comfortable and far more popular with passengers than any more recent bus design.

With the privatisation of London Buses in the 1990s, London Transport will continue to regulate bus services in London but has no responsibility for bus engineering and design. Current improvements to vehicle design, such

as low-floor buses which are easier for the elderly or disabled to use, are essentially adaptations of manufacturers' standard designs. The only central design control that will now remain with London Transport, perhaps because of a widely expressed view that it is part of London's heritage, is the

Above: FRM1, the unique front-entrance, rear-engine version of the Routemaster built in 1966, and destined to be the last bus designed specifically for London.

Left: RMC Green Line coach, 1962, a luxury development of the Routemaster with more comfortable seating, luggage racks, fluorescent lighting and distinctive twin headlamps.

familiar red livery. This will be kept on the central London routes currently operated by the London Buses companies, whoever they are owned by in the future.

Trams and Trolleybuses

Tramway mechanisation followed a quite different route to that of buses. Instead of a portable power source in each vehicle, electric tramways use centrally generated power fed to each tram on the network. This required substantial investment in an infrastructure of generating station, distribution system, track and power supply arrangements, none of which was needed for buses.

All but one of the electric tramway networks in London used the standard method of current collection from an overhead wire through a sprung trolley pole on the roof of the tram. The London County Council, which built the largest system in the capital, was unusual in adopting the conduit system where trams picked up the power from underground conductor rails laid in a channel below the tracks. Contact was made through a 'plough' mechanism carried underneath each vehicle, which fitted into the slot in the road surface between the rails. This system avoided the need for unsightly overhead wires but was expensive to build and maintain.

London's first electric services were introduced by the privately owned London United Tramways, which opened two routes running into the western suburbs from Shepherds Bush in 1901. Thirteen more separate electric tramway systems were opened in greater London over the next five years. Outside the London County Council boundary, operation was divided between three private companies in the northern, western and southern suburbs, and local authorities in east and south-east London. Between them these tramways were carrying

Above: London County Council Tramways No.1, 'Bluebird', the advanced prototype for a new class of trams that were never built, 1932.

over 800 million passengers a year by 1914, more than the total for the buses and Underground combined.

Like buses, early electric trams were similar in overall design to horse-drawn vehicles, but the potential for a dramatic increase in size with mechanisation was much greater. Metropolitan Police licensing regulations were as strict for trams as they were for buses, though they at least allowed covered top decks from an early stage. In every other respect the first generation of electric trams were spartan vehicles, offering cheap, rapid and frequent (sometimes all-night) services rather than comfort.

The London County Council Tramways department was an enormous and impressive operation, but design innovation was not one of its characteristics. The LCC operated well-tried, traditional equipment, relying on a high standard of construction and maintenance. By 1907 what was effectively a standard London tramcar design had been developed for the LCC and was also supplied by the manufacturers to four of the outer London council tramways. More than a thousand of these large double-deck cars, seating up to 73 passengers, were built to this basic design between 1907 and 1930. By the late 1920s the older vehicles required modernisation with enclosed platforms and upholstered seating – 'pullmanisation' as the LCC called it – to compete with the latest buses.

The fact that many Edwardian tramcars were still in service when London's tramways were finally abandoned in the early 1950s is a tribute to their robustness, but it also underlines the LCC's conservative approach. It was not until 1932 that the LCC finally got round to designing a completely new and advanced type of tram. 'Bluebird', as the dark blue prototype was nicknamed, was intended to be the first of a batch of one hundred luxury cars, but when London Transport took over a year later all tramway development

Left: August Bank Holiday at Shepherds Bush, 1903, with crowds boarding one of the London United Tramways' original open-top electric cars for a day out by the river at Hampton Court or Twickenham.

Below left: A busy traffic scene at Gardiner's Corner, Aldgate in 1912, dominated by large London County Council tramcars and one smaller West Ham Corporation car (second from the left). The open-top B type motor bus (centre right) seems tiny compared with the electric trams.

GREGORY
BROWN

KINGSTON

HX 12496

BY
TROLLEYBUS
TO
KINGSTON
OLD-WORLD MARKET-PLACE
RIVER-SIDE WALKS
BOATING BATHING

CHANGE AT WIMBLEDON
FOR THE TROLLEYBUSES

was abandoned. Car number 1, which still survives at the National Tramway Museum in Derbyshire, remains a unique example of what might have been.

It was the privately owned tramways, which had become part of the Underground Group, that led the way in developing new tramcar designs in the late 1920s. Until then it had been standard practice to build trams with heavy wooden-framed bodies – apart

from the all-steel cars designed for use in the Kingsway Tram Subway. The new streamlined Feltham cars built in 1930–31 for the Metropolitan Electric and London United Tramways had lightweight all-metal bodies and new features such as heaters, air-operated doors as on tube trains and fully sprung upholstered seating. The Felthams were reputedly the fastest trams in Europe, but they were to be the last of their kind in

London rather than the shape of things to come. In 1931, the year these luxurious new trams entered service, a Royal Commission on Tramways recommended that tramways should be gradually phased out. London Transport, which inherited all the London tramway undertakings in 1933, soon decided to follow this advice and replace its trams with trolleybuses.

A trolleybus is basically a cross between a tram and a bus. It is electrically powered, using an overhead supply, but instead of running on rails it has rubber-tyred wheels. This gives the trolleybus greater flexibility than the tram, allowing it to be driven to the kerbside at stops and manoeuvred to avoid obstructions in the road. The fixed nature of tram tracks, giving the vehicles enforced priority over all other road users, became one of the main arguments against trams in the 1930s, although in modern traffic management schemes it is often claimed as an advantage.

During the 1920s, London's tramways began to lose money. Passengers deserted them for the new buses, and the tramway operators could not afford the essential modernisation necessary to win back their customers. One company saw that the trolleybus offered a way out of its difficulties. The London United Tramways decided to invest in the new Feltham tramcars for its busiest routes but to convert others to trolleybus operation. New twin overhead wiring was required but the trolleybuses could use the same power-supply system as the trams, and the track, which was expensive to maintain, could be taken up.

In 1931, the LUT introduced trolleybuses over seventeen miles of former tram route in the Kingston area. The conversion was carried out at less than half the estimated cost of tramway modernisation. The trolleybuses also proved cheaper to run and soon attracted more passengers than the trams had carried. These original vehicles had AEC chassis with

bodies of similar appearance to the LGOC's motor buses of the period.

The LUT's successful experience in trolleybus operation led London Transport to plan further conversions. From 1935 to 1940, when the programme was interrupted by

the war, more than half London's tramways were converted to trolleybus operation. As Ashfield and Pick, the Chairman and Vice Chairman of the new Board, came from the Underground Group, whose road services were dominated by the LGOC's bus operations, it is perhaps not surprising that London Transport abandoned its tramway inheritance so quickly. Yet even Pick had some difficulties in fitting trolleybuses into his design philosophy. The problem was an unavoidable conflict between visual appearance and operational necessity. Trolleybuses need twice as much wiring as trams to provide a separate current return, and where they replaced the LCC conduit system it meant erecting wires where there had been none before. Pick asked Holden to design special poles to support the wiring which were as discreet as possible, but it was

Below: Trolleybuses at North Finchley in 1958, showing the complex and unsightly network of overhead wires required at a major intersection.

Opposite: (Top left) The all-metal body shells of Feltham tramcars under construction at the Union Construction and Finance Company works at Feltham, west London, 1930. (Far left) A sleek new London United Tramways Feltham car at Ealing Broadway in 1931 is an impressive contrast to the open-top LGOC bus beside it which dates from the early 1920s. (Left) A poster by Gregory Brown issued in 1933 which features one of the original London trolleybuses introduced two years earlier.

difficult to minimise the visual intrusion of the 'overhead'. At major intersections complicated networks of suspended points and cross-overs had to be put up. In a radio interview in 1933 about design in the street, Pick was asked to comment on 'all those posts

After the war there was less financial benefit in continuing to use the ageing tramway electrical distribution system than there had been in the 1930s. In 1946 London Transport announced that no further tram to trolleybus conversions would take place, and diesel buses were used to replace the remaining trams in 1950–52. Although the trolleybus network did not expand further, the number of vehicles grew to a peak of 1,811 in the early 1950s, then the largest trolleybus fleet in the world. Most of these were large 70-seat vehicles built to a standard basic design for London Transport by both AEC and Leyland.

The relative running costs of buses and trolleybuses were about equal at this time but there was a strong case for making one form of traction standard. A three-year 'buses for trolleybuses' replacement programme began in 1959 just before delivery of the new Routemaster buses began. The final stage, appropriately enough, covered the Kingston area served by the original LUT routes. London's last trolleybus ran to Fulwell Depot in the south-western suburbs on 8 May 1962.

Trolleybuses are unlikely to return to the streets of London but there has recently been a revival of interest in the tram in its modern 'light-rail' form. The Docklands Light Railway, opened in 1987, uses automated, driverless cars on a self-contained network that runs partly on the trackbeds of disused railway lines. London Transport operated the DLR until 1992, but was not involved in the design of the vehicles which are based on standard German light-rail units. Street-running trams will soon return to London with Tramlink, a new light-rail system planned for the Croydon area, but this will use modern 'supertrams' developed by manufacturers for general use on light-rail networks. They will not be designed specifically for London.

Above: Trolleybus production for London Transport was shared by AEC and Leyland. This illustration is taken from a Leyland brochure of 1936.

and wires tangled above its surface'. He replied that there was no need for them to be tangled: 'They can be tidy. Really well designed suspension is beautiful as a spider's web is beautiful.'

It was not a convincing argument, and London Transport faced many complaints when it sought permission to put up trolleybus wires in some of London's historic streets and squares. Before the design of the overhead was finalised Pick sent a memo to the general manager of trams and trolleybuses emphasising that 'very considerable importance attaches to our making this suspension as pleasing as we possibly can'. In the end he must have felt that they had failed in their task. It was a conflict where Pick's 'fitness for purpose' yardstick on design could not provide an appropriate solution to the problem.

Underground Trains

The City and South London Railway, opened in 1890, was the first underground electric railway in the world. It was also innovative in being constructed at deep level using a cylindrical tunnelling shield. The circular-profile tunnel was lined with curved cast-iron segments bolted together to form a tube of concentric rings – hence the name for these deep-level railways. Six more tube lines were opened in quick succession at the turn of the century, each started by a separate company although most of them soon became part of the Underground Group.

During the same period the existing underground lines of the Metropolitan and District Railways, which ran in shallow tunnels, were electrified to compete with the new tubes, although steam services continued on the outer main line of the Metropolitan. In less than twenty years electric travel underground, which had seemed a daring experiment in 1890, had become part of the daily routine for thousands of Londoners.

The tube railways brought many changes to the design of underground trains. The old steam underground lines were built to the same dimensions and loading gauge as overground railways, and used rolling stock of similar size and layout. Tube stock had to be much more compact to fit the smaller tunnels, which were just 10ft. (3.0m.) in diameter on the City and South London and 12ft. (3.6m.) on the other tube lines. Only the Great Northern and City line with 16ft. (4.88m.) tunnels was built to take rolling stock of main-line dimensions.

All the tube railways had just one class of travel and open saloon coaches without divided compartments. Seating was either cross-facing or mixed, following tramway rather than railway practice. Entrance and exit were through doors at either end of each car, outside which were open platforms. Gatemen let passengers on and off by opening and closing metal lattice gates on each end platform when the train had stopped. On the

original 'padded cell' cars of the City and South London, which had no windows, the gatemen also had to call out the station names, but all later tube stock had full-size windows. The City and South London and Central London tubes both began operations using electric locomotives to haul their trains. These were inconvenient for short, busy lines as it was necessary to run the locomotive round the train at the terminus before making a return journey. The solution was to adopt the multiple-unit control system devised by Frank Sprague in Chicago during the 1890s, which made locomotives redundant. Motors and control equipment were fitted to some of the passenger cars in the train, linked by a low-voltage control circuit. This allowed operation from one controller in the cab of the leading car. With a cab at both

Below left: Contemporary drawing of the original City and South London terminus at Stockwell, 1890. On the left is one of the 14 small locomotives built by Beyer Peacock with Mather and Platt electrical equipment. A train of 'padded cell' cars is on the right, with the metal lattice gates on the end platforms clearly visible.

Bottom: Advertising the new District Railway electric services, c1905. These American-style trains, known as B stock, were built in Britain, France and Belgium.

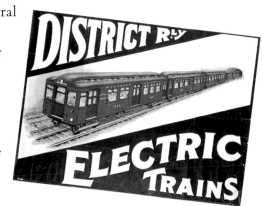

Above: Central London Railway multiple-unit stock, the first of its kind to operate in Britain, 1903.

E is for Energy of the kind called Electric,
And this is the house where the Engineer makes it.

ends of the train it could be driven in either direction like a tram.

In 1903 the Central London became the first railway in Britain to be worked entirely with multiple-unit trains and the system was subsequently adopted for all the other tube lines. Multiple-unit trains were also introduced on the Metropolitan and District Railways when they were electrified in 1905. These larger 'surface stock' trains had a distinctly American appearance with their open saloons and raised clerestory roof sections. The Metropolitan also introduced electric locomotives for use on long-distance trains which had to be hauled beyond the limits of electrification by steam locomotives. The locomotive-hauled trains used conventional passenger coaches whose only underground design feature was the curved shape to the top of the doors, intended to prevent them from hitting the tunnel wall if they should fly open while the train was between stations.

In 1902 the American financier Charles Tyson Yerkes founded the Underground Electric Railways Company of London Ltd (UERL), a holding company commonly known as the Underground Group. This expanded rapidly to take control of the District Railway and three new tube lines then under construction – the Bakerloo,

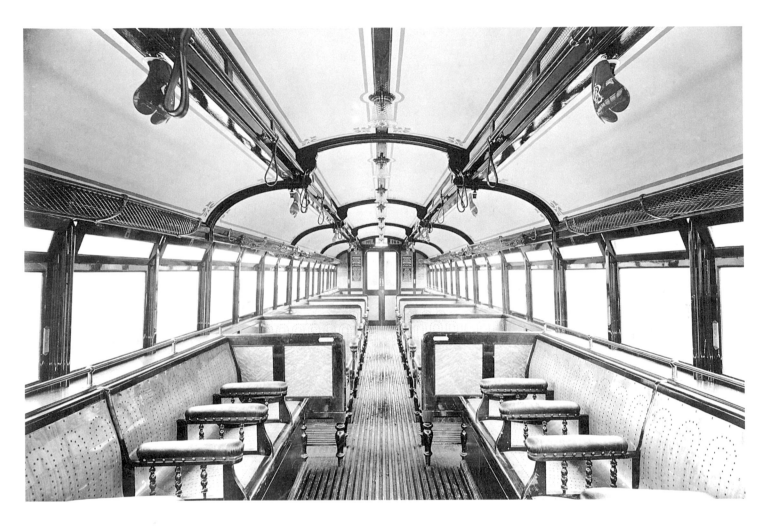

Piccadilly and Hampstead (now Northern Line) tubes, all opened in 1906–7. The rolling stock for the Underground Group's tubes was all of the same general design, despite being supplied by four different manufacturers. Although the early cars built for the Central London Railway had had wooden bodies, new Board of Trade fire precaution regulations stipulated all-steel construction and this became standard practice on underground trains.

It was hardly surprising, in view of the Underground Group's American financial backing and management, that American-influenced design and engineering was adopted both for the electrification of the District and for the three new tubes. The giant generating station built at Lots Road, Chelsea to supply all the lines was very similar to contemporary American power

houses. The four-rail arrangement for power pick up also followed American practice and enabled an automatic track circuit control system for the signalling pioneered on the Boston Elevated Railway to be adopted. American automatic couplers were fitted to all underground rolling stock and even American words like 'car', rather than the coach or carriage familiar on British railways, became standard Underground terminology. All these features were eventually applied to the other tube lines when they became part of the Underground Group.

As operations expanded in the 1920s, with new lines extending into the suburbs, there was a progressive move towards standardisation of new rolling stock and modernisation or replacement of the old. A large central repair depot for heavy overhaul was opened at Acton in 1922 on an adjacent

Above: The interior of an open saloon car on the Central London Railway, 1900. Unlike the overground railways, tube travel was classless, with the same fare and accommodation for all passengers.

Far left: The 'Chelsea Monster', Lots Road Power Station, opened in 1905. At the time it was the largest electrical generating station in Europe. Illustration from Charles Pears' children's alphabet of 1914.

Right: Cutaway diagram showing the body frame construction of the original motor cars used on the three Underground Group tubes – the Bakerloo, Piccadilly and Hampstead lines. They were all very similar in design though built by five different manufacturers in Britain, France, Hungary and the United States.

Below: An Underground poster by R.T. Cooper issued in 1924 illustrating the transformation from the old City and South London Railway, seen as a ghostly apparition on the right, to the reconstructed line on the left with new air door Standard stock.

site to the LGOC's Chiswick bus works, and a 'flowline' overhaul procedure similar to that used on the buses was introduced for Underground trains. This involved attaching vehicles to a continuous cable which moved them slowly through the workshops like a factory production line.

The recognisable characteristics of modern London Underground trains – several air-operated sliding doors to each car and comfortable cushion seats covered in woollen moquette fabric – appeared in the Standard stock cars introduced in the early 1920s. By 1930 all the original gate stock trains had been modernised or replaced. These developments were not merely technical advances. They reflected Pick's belief that the organisation should be constantly improving the design and efficiency of its products and services. With his elevation to Joint Assistant

Managing Director in 1921, Pick was able to apply his design management philosophy more broadly and to influence areas such as rolling stock design rather than just publicity. 'To those who know and use the Underground Railways, the impression must always be dynamic,' he wrote in 1928 after his promotion to Managing Director.

The dynamism was not just window dressing or, in modern jargon, marketing hype, however. Pick's vision of the Underground as the modern, pulsating heart of civilised urban society meant that he expected high standards and commitment from his colleagues and staff:

They are not required to come into the machinery merely to keep it turning. There is no real education in that. They are expected to continue those adjustments and

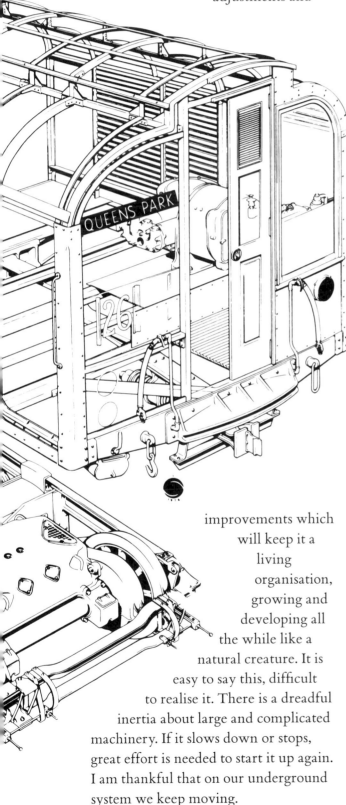

improvements which will keep it a living organisation, growing and developing all the while like a natural creature. It is easy to say this, difficult to realise it. There is a dreadful inertia about large and complicated machinery. If it slows down or stops, great effort is needed to start it up again. I am thankful that on our underground system we keep moving.

These comments come from Pick's foreword to a book by the Underground's Operating Manager, J.P Thomas, called *Handling London's Underground Traffic*, published in 1928. Thomas's matter-of-fact description of the Underground's complex operations shows the Pick philosophy in action, at once wide-ranging and incredibly detailed. Take, for instance, this description of the interior design of District Railway cars:

After the 1920 stock had been in service a year or so it was thought that the all-steel construction produced a cold appearance, and steps were taken to brighten up the cars. The services of a prominent artist were obtained to plan colour schemes for the interiors and the upholstery was altered to match. In the latest design of cars a number of fittings have been introduced for the purpose of noise reduction and to give the cars a warmer appearance.

Only Pick would have gone to these lengths, which involved bringing in an expert in acoustics to study the problem of noise in trains, and devising a new design of removable seat cushion which was both more comfortable and more easily cleaned.

Pick's approach, which became the Underground's corporate philosophy, meant a continuous striving for better quality and the raising of

Above: Overhaul of original District Railway electric stock at Mill Hill Park Works in about 1910, before the concentration of the Underground's heavy repair facilities at Acton Works in the 1920s.

Below: Professor Low with his audiometer conducting experiments to reduce the noise of trains at Acton Works, 1922.

QUICKLY AWAY, THANKS TO
DOORS
PNEUMATIC

The doors, which are edged with rubber, are kept closed by air-engine arms, one for each door.

The arms engage in slots in the doors, which open when the arms swing round. The doors are held open by the arms. The signal to start cannot be given while the doors are open.

Above: Poster by Laszlo Moholy-Nagy, 1938, showing the workings of air doors which were a standard feature of all tube stock by this date.

standards. The sliding pneumatic doors are an example of an innovation which would have been judged successful only because it met a range of strict requirements. The doors saved time because the new trains had more doors and passengers could get on and off more quickly. They saved money because they required only one guard to control a whole train and did not need gatemen. They were convenient and easy for passengers. Finally, they were based on thoroughly tested and

reliable technology. This was 'fitness for purpose' applied with a vengeance!

Until the mid-1920s it was the Underground Group's usual practice to lay down general specifications for its rolling-stock requirements but to leave the design details to the suppliers. As the company began to develop its own experimental and research facilities at Acton, it became more demanding and specific in its orders. In 1928 the Underground Group even began building its own new trains through a subsidiary company, the Union Construction and Finance Company, set up at Feltham in west London. The UCC also built the new Feltham tramcars and the bodies for the original London United Tramways trolleybuses. Loud complaints from other train builders at this move towards monopoly supply arrangements by the Underground Group led to the winding up of the UCC in 1933, and the prohibition of future manufacturing by London Transport on the railway side under the terms of its constitution in 1933.

The Metropolitan Railway, which remained independent of the Underground Group until the forced amalgamation into London Transport, took a very different approach. The Metropolitan had long been a strangely mixed railway with two very different operations – on the one side a long-distance main line into the country with fast passenger and goods trains, and on the other an intensively worked urban electric underground system. The company's rolling stock policy was as inconsistent as this diversity of operations. There were both steam and electric locomotives, multiple-unit and locomotive-hauled stock, and within each group a range of incompatible electrical equipment, braking systems and couplers. Occasionally there was a flash of innovation, such as a pioneering introduction of roller bearings on some new stock in 1929, which saved on lubrication and eliminated the

Above: Artwork by Lightfoot for a New Works poster, 1932. It captures perfectly the dynamic, progressive and ever improving image of the Underground which Pick wished to promote.

Left: A 1923 Standard stock train at Hendon Central soon after the opening of the Edgware extension in 1924.

common problem of overheating axle boxes. Overall, however, the Metropolitan's eccentricities and traditionalism, which were typical of most long-established railway companies, were the antithesis of the ordered, progressive approach of the Underground.

London Transport

Inevitably it was the systematic philosophy of the Underground Group that was inherited by London Transport, and after 1933 the wayward Metropolitan was gradually integrated with the rest of the Underground's practices. The 1935–40 New Works Programme, which involved extending the Bakerloo, Northern and Central Lines, led London Transport to develop an advanced new standard tube train. Four experimental six-car trains were built by Metropolitan-Cammell and delivered for trial running in 1936. The trains incorporated a number of design modifications and improvements, the most important being the relocation of all control gear under the floor. On the driving motor cars of the existing Standard stock, a large compartment behind each cab was taken up with this equipment. By making this space available for passenger seating, it was possible to increase the carrying capacity of a train by 14 per cent.

Three of the four trains had fully streamlined cab ends, but this fashionable 1930s feature was soon found to be of little benefit at the relatively low speeds reached by tube trains. The curve of the cab ends also wasted some of the space gained by using underfloor control equipment, and the centrally placed driver's seat hindered emergency exit and was disliked by motormen. On the fourth train the cab ends were flat with only a slight curve on the sides and on the roof. This was the design adopted for the subsequent production cars and it remained the standard outline shape of London tube trains for nearly half a century. A total of 1,121 new cars, known as 1938 tube stock, were subsequently ordered from the Metropolitan-Cammell and Birmingham Railway Carriage and Wagon companies, the first train entering passenger service on the Northern Line in June 1938. They were designed for a maximum 40-year life

Right: Experimental 1935 stock on trial in 1936. It was soon discovered that full streamlining was of little benefit at the low speeds reached by tube trains.

Overleaf: The classic 1938 stock which set the design style of tube trains for nearly fifty years. Some of them are still in use on the Isle of Wight.

expectancy but in fact the last '38 stock was withdrawn from service in its Golden Jubilee year, 1988, and some of the trains are still in use with new owners and new liveries, providing the main rail service on the Isle of Wight.

Responsibility for the design of this highly advanced and exceptionally durable rolling stock in the 1930s lay with W.S. Graff-Baker, who became Chief Mechanical Engineer (Railways) for London Transport in 1935. As well as the 1938 tube stock, Graff-Baker's team at Acton produced a striking new design for surface stock trains to the larger dimensions suitable for the District, Circle and Metropolitan Lines. A total of 573 O, P and Q stock cars, all of similar appearance, were built by the Gloucester and Birmingham companies to London Transport's specifications in 1936–40. Their most distinctive design feature was a flared base to the smooth exterior body line which incorporated the door step and was intended to prevent passengers from jumping on to a

moving train and forcing open the doors. This was a dangerous but common practice on the older trains with manually operated sliding doors, which had an alarming habit of sliding open of their own accord while the train was in motion. The first of these sleek (and much safer) new trains entered service on the Hammersmith and City Line early in 1937.

The interior design of London Transport's new Underground stock in the 1930s received as much care and attention as its mechanical engineering and body structure. Lighting levels were increased but with the glare of naked light bulbs diffused by elegant art deco glass shades. These would not have looked out of place in a restaurant or hotel lounge, although London Transport staff always referred to them prosaically as 'shovel shades'. Rush-hour standing passengers now had flexible moulded rubber hand grips instead of leather straps to hang on to. These proved an ideal design for another quite unpredicted purpose when they were issued to commando troops during the war as coshes.

Right: Flare-sided surface stock for the District, Circle and Metropolitan Lines introduced in 1937.

Left and below: 1938 stock interior with detail showing the elegant 'shovel shade' lighting and flexible moulded rubber hand grips for standing passengers.

For passengers who did get a seat there were further improvements to the design of the cushions and seat backs which were as comfortable as any first-class accommodation on a main-line express train. Unlike most metro systems where very basic hard seating is standard, London Transport has always

Above: The trim shop at Acton Works in 1939 where seat cushions were cleaned, repaired and recovered.

maintained a high level of comfort with seats covered in hard-wearing woollen moquette fabric. In the 1920s the fabric designs were taken from manufacturers' standard ranges, but by the 1930s Pick wanted new designs created specially for London Transport's buses and trains. He commissioned three artist-designers – Enid Marx, Marion Dorn and Paul Nash – to come up with something more inspired than the fabrics the suppliers were offering. The designs of all three were used, but it was Enid Marx who found this unusual industrial textile design commission particularly interesting and useful experience when she later worked on utility textile designs during the war:

My own first effort at designing for the L.P.T.B. was when Christian Barman (the Publicity Officer) invited me to design the seating material for the inside of the trains. Barman's brief was very much to the point. It started off by informing me that some of the trains started in the country, in daylight, and then went on underground and this fact meant that careful consideration had to be given to the colour or colours used in the interiors of the trains, particularly for the seating, as certain colours responded well to daylight but not nearly so well when going underground into artificial light. Because of this, for a start, he had chosen green as his main colour for the seating materials. The second thing was that owing to the very hard wear the seats were subjected to, he chose a moquette which is an extremely hard-wearing form of velveteen, cut and uncut according to the brief given to the manufacturers. The cut, or velvet, surface was pleasanter to sit on, but the uncut looped weave was interspersed in order to make the material more hard-wearing. I enquired about the scale of the seating but I gathered it varied and I really had to ignore this when thinking about the size of the repeats. The important thing about the design as a whole was to remember, first, that occasionally the seating would not be seen in the rush hour and then there would be gaps and people would be sitting opposite an empty seat, and therefore you had to remember not to produce a design which could in any way be dazzling or give the passenger a feeling of sea-sickness. The other important item from the point of view of design was to remember that the variation of class of customer was very wide. You got dustmen and people doing outside and dirty work going by train from job to job, you also had ladies in fine clothes going to parties and not wanting to sit on a dust heap. So one had, as a designer, to remember this and design using a variation of tone which helped give

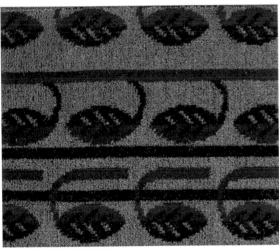 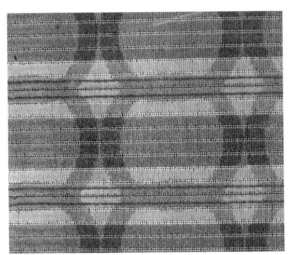

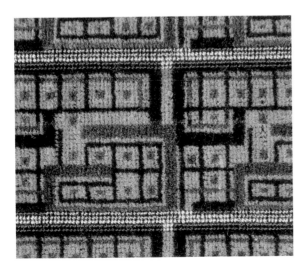 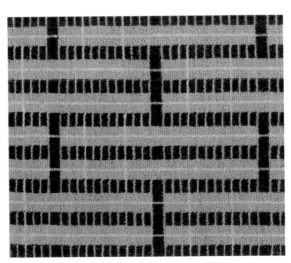

Left: Designs for Underground seating in woollen moquette by Enid Marx (top), Marion Dorn (centre) and Paul Nash (bottom), 1936–46.

the effect of a clean seat. In fact, variation of tone was far more important than the use of one or more than one colour. Finally, Christian Barman informed me that the problem with the seating in the Underground was not only to look fresh but also that certain areas of the seat, where the behind went and where the back rubbed would wear more than the rest of the area covered by the moquette.

Right: A train of R stock, the first unpainted aluminium Underground cars, introduced on the District Line in 1953.

Below: Graffiti cleaning. This process can damage the bodywork of unpainted trains, and the problem led to the decision to paint all Underground stock in a new livery in the 1990s.

London Transport's experience in aircraft construction during the war, when it was involved in building over 700 Halifax heavy bombers, contributed to the most significant design development in Underground trains in the early post-war years. This was the extensive use of lightweight aluminium alloys in body and underframe construction which improved efficiency by reducing the weight and, because aluminium does not rust, introduced the age of the unpainted silver train. London Transport's first silver R stock car was ready for display at the Festival of Britain in 1951, and the first complete silver train entered service on the District Line in 1953. All new trains ordered since have been largely of aluminium construction and were left unpainted until the New York fashion for

Right: 1973 stock on the
Piccadilly Line (left) and
D78 stock on the District
Line at Hammersmith,
showing the difference
in size between tube and
surface stock trains.

Below: Artist's
impression of the new
tube trains for the
Victoria Line styled by
Design Research Unit,
1967.

spray-canning trains with graffiti 'tags' hit London in the 1980s. London Underground suddenly found itself spending more than two million pounds a year cleaning defaced trains, and the acid scouring was damaging the bodywork of the rolling stock. It was decided to revert to painting all trains, which makes graffiti cleaning easier, and this has combated a very damaging 'hobby' which makes the travelling environment of the Underground threatening for passengers.

In the early 1960s London Transport experimented with automatic driving equipment for trains, and the Victoria Line, which opened in 1968–9, was the first automatic underground railway in the world. The train operator acts as both driver and guard, opening and closing the doors, then pressing two start buttons which activate the automatic control mechanism. Acceleration and braking are controlled by coded electrical impulse commands passed through the running rails. A manual over-ride facility is incorporated but is not generally required

during normal operation. Full automation of this kind has not been adopted on any of the other Underground lines, although all new trains delivered since 1968 have been suitable for driver-only operation without a guard.

The new Victoria Line trains concealed their advanced technology under a conventional exterior which kept to the overall profile of the 1938 stock but was crisply styled by a design consultancy, the

Design Research Unit, with twin headlamps and wrap-around cab windows. For the first and, so far, only time in the history of London Underground the appearance of the rolling stock was an integral part of the design package the Design Research Unit provided for the whole railway, and the trains echo the slightly clinical silver and grey colours reflected throughout the line in the escalators, ticket machines, automatic fare collection barriers and other hardware. The interior layout of the trains remained similar to the pre-war style but with various new materials; plastic laminates and metal replaced wood, double glazing gave better sound insulation, new dual-level armrests were made of fibreglass and, as in all new trains since the 1950s, there was fluorescent lighting throughout, creating a brighter but visually harsher travelling environment.

London Transport's international pre-eminence in the design and engineering of underground trains has been largely lost since the 1960s as new and more advanced metro systems have been built all over the world. For example, London Underground has been slow to adopt technological advances such as solid state 'chopper' traction control equipment now widely used elsewhere. To some extent innovation has been curtailed by Government limitations on the finance available for investment in new trains. However, unlike the privatised London bus companies, who are operators only, buying in 'off-the-peg' vehicles with only marginal design adaptations, London Underground will inevitably continue to have a significant input into train design because there is no such thing as an 'off-the-peg' tube train. Their rolling stock will always be uniquely designed for London.

In 1993 the first in a new generation of trains entered service on the Central Line. Known as the 1992 stock these trains have bodyshells fabricated from long welded aluminium extrusions which are lighter and stronger than previous designs. A new traction

Above and right: 1992 tube stock for the Central Line designed by David Carter Associates (DCA). The externally hung doors and uneven window alignment give these trains a rather clumsy external appearance.

control system allows much better acceleration and braking, while the use of air bag secondary suspension gives an improved ride quality even at higher speeds. The trains look different on the outside, having externally hung doors with a double width of 1,664mm., 314mm. wider than existing 1962 Central Line stock. This allows improved passenger flow on and off trains. The cars have large windows that are rolled over on to the roof,

giving greater visibility for passengers. Car ends also have large windows giving a more open, modern appearance. This is slightly spoilt by the considerable difference in height between the driving cab windows and the rest of the car, which is visually jarring.

The prime task for the designer was to maximise the internal space in the cars: there are 300 seats in an eight-car train compared with 328 in the 1962 stock, giving greater floor space and standing capacity. Total loading is nearly 1,700 seated and standing passengers per train, as opposed to 1,360 for the older trains. Internally the all-longitudinal seating is arranged with the seats set back in the centre of the car to allow greater standing room, and to encourage passengers to move down the car. There are also benches in the car ends on which standing passengers can perch. Windows in the end of the cars allow a view right through the train, promoting a feeling of safety. Grab poles are well sited and coloured red for ease of identification. An updated version of the traditional moquette is used on the seats, but patterned polymer is used for the floor for the first time rather than traditional slatted maple.

The train was created from three prototypes, which were developed and tested during 1986–88. The final design, built by ABB Transportation, incorporates the lessons learned from all three. The 1992 stock is the first in which London Underground has used an industrial design consultant (DCA Design of Warwick) to draw up concepts for a complete train; the result is only partially successful. Certainly the attention given to the driver's cab provides a much improved ergonomic design, and the interior layout works well, as do the large windows and improved car-to-car visibility. However, some aspects of the design are less satisfactory. The lighting is poorly detailed and provides very spotty illumination of line diagrams; the seating is hard and seems badly proportioned, and the red-painted handrails give a confused appearance to the interior. On the outside the train is well detailed but suffers from the imposition of a livery which serves only to break up its lines even more than the inevitable clumsiness of the externally hung doors. In all, it is a business-like train, but lacks the elegance of some of its predecessors.

At the same time as the design and testing programme for the '92 stock was progressing to a conclusion, a separate programme of refurbishing existing stock started. The impetus for this came from the Fennel Report on the 1987 King's Cross disaster. Fennel required London Underground to remove all non fire-safe materials from trains and the opportunity was taken to embark on an ambitious programme of interior redesign. This covered all interior elements and the refurbished trains have a completely new feel.

The basic interior colour is ivory, applied to light-gauge vitreous enamel and composite melamine panelling, to give a light, bright appearance to trains that were previously a drab grey. Flooring has been changed to a coloured composite rubber compound with profiled ribbing. All the refurbished trains have seating moquettes in the tradition of the classic designs produced before the war by people such as Enid Marx. Colours reflect the line colour. New lighting by profiled luminaires provides a much more even spread of light than the new Central Line stock; the additional brightness contributes substantially to a more welcoming and less threatening ambience. Perhaps the least successful aspect of the design is the attempt to provide a link to the line colours through the grab rails. One or two are successful, notably the Circle Line with its cheerful yellow, and the Bakerloo rich brown which seems to tie together the whole interior. The others are less successful and in the later refurbishments attempts are being made to provide bright contrasting handrails without a line parentage.

The refurbishment programme has provided some very successful updates of the existing stock, and has made use of some of the lessons learned in developing the 1992 stock, notably in lighting and moquettes, as well as much interior detailing such as

draught screens. The original trains, having been designed at different times between the early 1960s and the 1970s, always had different interior treatments. They now have greater consistency, but the opportunity has been missed to produce a strong corporate interior based on a limited palette and a number of repeatable proven design elements.

Above and left: Carefully planned refurbishment of old trains can sometimes produce better quality second time round. The dull and unattractive C stock introduced on the Hammersmith and City, Circle and District Lines in the 1970s (left) has been improved dramatically with a radical interior refit in the 1990s.

Information and publicity in London Transport follow a tradition created almost single-handedly by Frank Pick. So many roads lead back to Pick that it can sometimes appear as though London Transport would not have existed without him. This would be to exaggerate his influence in many areas, but not as far as publicity

Below: Cover to the original hardback edition of *Visitor's London,* 'an alphabetical reference book for the visitor to London who wishes also to see something of London's countryside' by Harold Hutchison, London Transport's Publicity Officer, published in 1954.

and information are concerned. Pick's understanding of the benefits of good publicity and the importance of clear communication was unique. The use of the best graphic designers, artists and typographers created at London Transport what the critic Nikolaus Pevsner called 'the most efficacious centre of visual education in England'. The tradition was so strong that over fifty years after Pick's death, programmes such as the present 'Art on the Underground', which in other companies would be considered extraordinarily daring, are taken for granted.

Above: An illustration from Charles Pears' *Alphabet of T.O.T.,* published by the Underground in 1914.

Opposite: Examples of recent London Transport publicity and information.

M is the Map which will make every way
Of the mighty Metropolis plain as the day.

UNDERGROUND

GROUND

VISITOR'S
LONDON

Bus Information

Clear and concise information has always been the key to persuading people to use buses. This information, whether contained on maps, timetables or marketing promotions, is essential to the irregular bus user if he or she is to unravel the labyrinthine London bus network. At the front of every bus traveller's mind are three questions: Where am I now? How do I get from here to where I want to go? How will I know when I have got there? This last is a particular worry in unfamiliar territory. Many attempts have been made to simplify and clarify the material, but the basic problem has usually been lack of co-ordination between the various elements. Maps were redesigned, timetables were not. Promotional material was rethought but bus-stop material was not. The result was never the co-ordinated and harmonious exercise in public information that it ought to have been.

The first London bus map, issued free by the London General Omnibus Company in 1911, was easy to read because it showed fewer than thirty routes. As services expanded, the map grew increasingly complex. By the 1950s, when services were at their peak, the London-wide bus map had become a masterpiece of cartographic ingenuity, but was of doubtful value as an information system. Very few people use buses to travel long distances across London, and the map was probably more help to the bus enthusiast who wanted to go everywhere by bus than to the typical passenger. Most London bus routes are long and tortuous, following no obvious logic other than the unplanned sprawl of the city itself. The urban geography of London allows little scope for simplifying the map into something like the straightforward uptown/downtown grid of New York City. Even tourists can hardly go wrong taking a bus in Manhattan, but most Londoners have never grasped the complexities of their own bus routes, even though many have not changed in over eighty years.

Right: The first LGOC bus map, issued in 1911, featured only 23 routes. The competitive slogans 'Travel Above Ground' and 'Open Air to Everywhere' were quickly abandoned when the company became part of the Underground Group a year later.

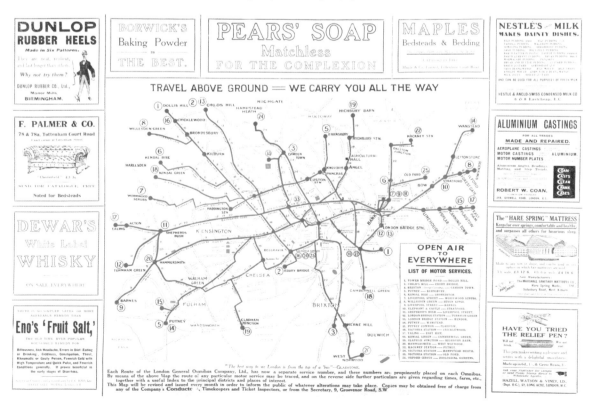

Left: An LGOC Birmingham Guild cast-iron bus stop of 1921 (left) and London Transport terrazzo finish concrete post with simplified enamel flag introduced in 1937 (right).

Below: New aluminium post bus stop designed by John Elson Design in 1992. This incorporates a cable duct to carry power to illuminate the timetables. Also shown is the redesigned route information by Fitch RS.

Bus stops first appeared in 1919, but a comprehensive system of compulsory and request stopping places was not set up by London Transport until the late 1930s. Until then it was theoretically possible to hail a bus anywhere, just like a taxi. Early bus-stop poles were green-painted cast-iron designs by the Birmingham Guild, some of which still survive on the streets. They were superseded in the early 1930s by cast-concrete posts made in London Transport's own building workshops at Parsons Green. The design soon evolved into a rather elegant streamlined shape finished in polished aggregate with a built-in timetable and information board. The flag design was also standardised in the late 1930s by Hans Schleger into an enamel square with the London Transport symbol and Johnston lettering. These simple pieces of street furniture literally flag up the whole

of London Transport's extensive bus-route network clearly and unobtrusively. Bus stops did not change a great deal over the next fifty years but their effectiveness as information points was diminished by inadequate or vandalised timetable boards and the replacement of the neat 'E' plate enamel route number slots with a rash of multi-coloured stickers.

London Transport has recently embarked on a comprehensive redesign of all bus-related material, from the bus map to the bus-stop flags. This will signal the end of the curious design known as the 'squirkle' map in which bus numbers were grouped together at nodal points in 'rounded squares'. This style defeated most users but remained current for nearly ten years. The review of information was made necessary partly by the change in status of the bus companies. The ten bus subsidiaries were privatised at the end of 1994 leaving London Transport as the regulatory body responsible for planning, infrastructure and information. Clearly, under the new arrangements, route changes, in response to competition pressures, will be greater; information including the bus-stop flags will need to be more flexible and responsive. The new designs by Fitch RS are clear and simple and go a long way towards solving the problem. Time will tell whether they encourage more people to use buses and whether they survive well-intentioned 'tinkering' over the next few years.

Underground Information

Visitors' maps of London featuring the Victorian steam underground lines were published by the District Railway as early as the 1880s and sold through stationers. After the electrification of the Metropolitan and District Railways and the opening of the six new tube lines, the various companies produced a joint London Underground

Railways map in folding pocket format which was issued free from 1908. A geographically accurate reproduction of all the lines laid over a central London street map was possible because the system was still fairly compact at this time. Only the outer overground sections of the Metropolitan and District Railways had to be excluded. By the 1920s the background street plans had been dropped and the map was being printed on more substantial card that folded neatly in three. The design, by the Underground's draughtsman F.H. Stingemore, was still geographical, but as new suburban extension lines were added it became increasingly difficult to fit the whole network on to a small-format map.

In 1931 Harry Beck, a young draughtsman working for the Underground, came up with a radical solution to the problem. In his spare time Beck had redesigned the map as a diagram, completely abandoning geographical accuracy for the sake of clarity. His layout, apparently inspired by electrical circuit diagrams, showed the various lines as

Right: The first London Underground Railways folding pocket map, issued free in 1908 (left) and the late 1920s version designed by F.H. Stingemore (right).

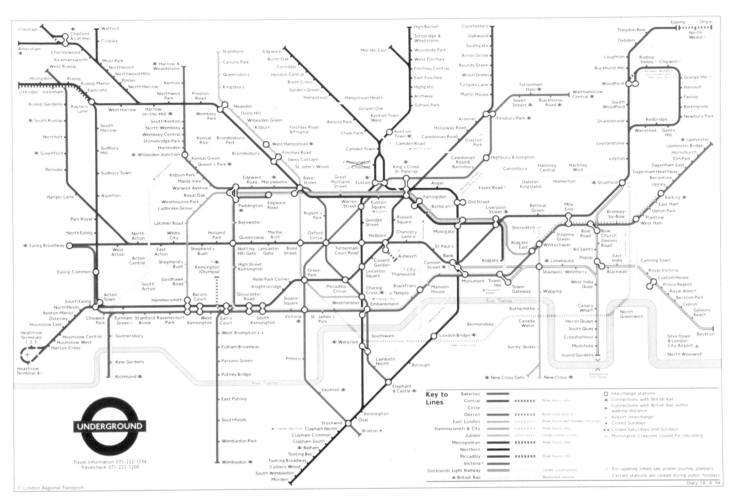

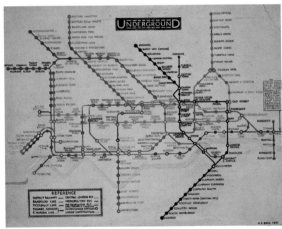

Above and left:
Presentation artwork
by Harry Beck for
his diagrammatic
Underground map,
1931 (above) and the first
printed version issued in
1933 (above left).

Top: The modern
Journey Planner, as the
map is now described,
still follows the Beck
format.

Below left: Finchley
Road Metropolitan
Railway station in
1910 swamped by
crude, oversized and
inappropriate signage,
none of which even gives
the name of the station.

Below right: The new
façade to the rebuilt
Hammersmith station by
Charles Holden, 1932,
could not be more
different. The simple
house style, Johnston
lettering and bar and
circle symbol announce
discreetly but clearly that
this is an Underground
station entrance.

verticals, horizontals and 45-degree diagonals.
The central area, which contains the most
complicated interchanges, was enlarged in
relation to the outer areas, making the whole
map much easier to read. Anyone who has
struggled with the complexities of the current
Paris Metro map will realise what a brilliantly
simple concept Beck designed for the London
Underground over sixty years ago.

Beck's unsolicited idea was tested by the
Underground in 1933, initially as a folding
pocket map which carried a note asking the
public for their comments. It was an instant
success with passengers, and London
Transport adopted the Beck format for their
large station wall maps as well as pocket
versions. Beck continued to experiment with
and adapt his design until the late 1950s,
but these and all subsequent versions of the
diagram have followed his original concept.
It has inspired numerous imitations, and the
diagrammatic map is now a standard means
of representing transport systems all over the
world. The Beck map, although not originally

commissioned by the Underground, is
perhaps the most influential London
Transport design of all.

Signage

The prime functions of signage are to inform
and reassure; however, these simple functions
are often lost in the overlay of other uses that
are given or ascribed to it. From corporate
identity and ownership, through to
marketing, signage is made to work hard for
its living, and London Transport's signage is
no different. Like most of London Transport's
infrastructure, it has developed from the
needs and identity of various companies that
came together over a period of forty years.
That so much of it speaks with a common
language is a tribute to Pick and others
who saw the benefits of a consistent voice,
and brought order into the chaos that had
previously existed.

The consistency of the signage is also a
tribute to the excellence of Johnston's typeface
which draws together an amazing diversity of

Left: New platform signage in the Johnston typeface at Leicester Square station after reconstruction, 1935. The 'bifurcation sign', to use London Transport's official description, faces the steps from the escalator landing and is clear enough to be read by an approaching passenger on the move. The only superfluous information is the platform number, which was later generally replaced by the direction of travel (eg. eastbound/ westbound).

Below right: St John's Wood, Metropolitan Railway, 1933. A real challenge to the passenger trying to identify the name of the station from a moving train! Pick may well have had this photographed to show how not to do it. On the Underground he always insisted on a grid system for the platform walls so that commercial advertising was kept separate from, and did not obscure, important signage and travel information.

Below: The distinctive flighted arrow roundel introduced on London Transport directional signs in the 1930s.

signage types and conventions. Over a period of sixty years the typeface was used in different weights with different spacing, on a bewildering collection of hardware, and was even redrawn as a serif face by Percy J. Delf Smith, and yet still the clarity showed through. At its best the signage had an elegance and clarity that was quite exceptional. When properly spaced and used in conjunction with the flighted arrow or the roundel, the Johnston letter form became 'London's handwriting'.

By the early 1980s, however, the poor standard of signage, particularly on the Underground, threatened finally to destroy the integrity of the typeface. Not only was there a bewildering array of different styles of sign, but from lack of proper direction signage became ill-ordered and confusing. If there is one thing worse than a total absence of signage, it is a plethora of signs saying the same thing in different ways. The problem was recognised in 1984 when a major study was commissioned from Henrion Ludlow and Schmidt. Their brief was to recommend courses of action to restore clarity and logic to the Underground signage without destroying its character. The recommendations were for a major programme of redesign and new signage based on the Banks and Miles face New Johnston. The results of this are now beginning to be seen on the system; based on strict hierarchies and firm principles, the new signage is introducing clarity, simplicity and consistency, though whether it will have the character and beauty of the 1930s work seems doubtful.

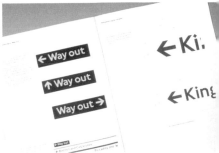

Above: Pages from the *London Underground Signing Manual* by Henrion Ludlow and Schmidt.

Left: Platform wall at Bethnal Green station, designed in the late 1930s but not opened until after the war. Advertising and travel information are clearly separated, to the benefit of both. Illustration by John See for the *London Underground Heritage Signing Manual*, 1993, also by Henrion Ludlow and Schmidt.

The development of the staff magazine. Covers of *T.O.T.* from 1925 (right), *Pennyfare* from 1937 (top right) and *London Lines* from 1994 (above).

Internal Communication

It is not only in communicating with passengers and the public that London Transport has established a tradition of excellence. For many years its internal communications to staff have been of very high quality. These communications have covered widely different subjects, from direct messages from the Chairman through newspapers and magazines to staff-training manuals.

A staff magazine called *T.O.T.* (which stood for Train, Omnibus, Tram) was started by the Underground Group as early as 1913. When London Transport was created in 1933, the magazine became *Pennyfare* and in 1947 was changed again to the *London Transport*

Magazine. In the 1970s the magazine was turned into a monthly newspaper, *LT News*, joined in the 1980s by *Tubeline.* Since 1990 an additional glossy quarterly magazine for senior staff and 'opinion formers' called *London Lines* has been published on London Transport's behalf. It is similar in format to many corporate magazines, with a high-quality design and layout.

During the last few years London Transport has produced some very interesting and innovative corporate identity manuals intended to be read as a background to the subject, as well as to provide information and guidance to the user. Among these are *Trains are for People, How to Use the London Transport Corporate Identity*, and *How to Use and Protect the Intellectual Property Rights of London Transport.* These manuals are now being widely copied by other companies as examples of a different way of communicating a difficult subject.

Johnston Typeface

One of the most important tools London Transport has had for conveying information clearly is its own unique typeface. The importance of Edward Johnston, the designer of the standard London Transport typeface, was that he almost single-handedly rediscovered the tools and techniques of calligraphy. His book *Writing and Illuminating and Lettering*, first published in 1906, was the benchmark for all future calligraphers and typographers. That he should have been selected by Frank Pick to design a letter face for an industrial enterprise was curious indeed, for Johnston disliked industry and all methods of mechanical reproduction. It is almost inconceivable that he could have embarked on the production of a sans serif letter face for an enterprise such as the Underground Group without recognising the likely outcome. Perhaps he saw no further than the immediate commission to provide a letter form for station names and display

purposes. The innovatory and influential typeface he created, however, has since been used in almost every possible configuration and tortured into uses of which he would hardly approve.

Johnston designed his original Underground lettering in 1916 for very limited applications and agonised over every

ODBEFHIJKLMN PQURSTVWCG QU WA &YXZJ

subsequent commission he undertook to enlarge or expand his family of typefaces. Pick wanted a design with, as he put it, 'the bold simplicity of the authentic lettering of the finest periods' and yet 'belonging unmistakably to the twentieth century'. Johnston had made a detailed study of early letter forms and met Pick's requirements by turning to classical Roman capitals for his inspiration and proportions. Once these had been established, the Underground face, he claimed, 'designed itself'. It is based on squares and circles, Johnston's O being a perfect circle and his capital M a square with the diagonal strokes meeting precisely in the centre of the letter. All strokes are of exactly the same weight.

The Johnston typeface was a copyright design for the exclusive use of the Underground Group, but imitations soon

Above: The Underground letter face hand drawn with detailed footnotes by Edward Johnston himself.

Below: Bar and circle nameplate with lettering and proportions to Edward Johnston's own final design, 1930s.

followed at home and abroad. Its major
progeny in Britain was Gill Sans, designed by
artist craftsman Eric Gill for the Monotype
Corporation in 1928. Gill Sans was adopted
by the London and North Eastern Railway
for all its signage, and the lettering soon
became a standard printer's typeface

Clarity of information on
the street. The Johnston
typeface used on a bus
stop and bus destination
blind at Waterloo in
1950 (left) and on station
signage at South Harrow
in 1935 (right).

throughout the industry. Gill had been a
pupil of Johnston and freely acknowledged
that his own much better known typeface
was in fact a close variant on Johnston's
classic Underground design.

The genius of Johnston's letter form lay
in its ability to survive adaptation and
change in a way that most other typefaces,
with the exception of Gill Sans, could not.
Some of the less successful variations were
designed by Johnston himself, such as the
condensed bus destination board lettering
of 1919 and the Underground bold of 1929.
Johnston also redesigned the proportions
of the standard Underground bull's-eye for
station nameplates to take his lettering.
But other variants were adaptations by
London Transport's staff which resulted in
a family of 'nearly Johnston' typefaces being
used for years without question. Despite

becoming synonymous with a great transport
company, the original Johnston face was
never applied universally throughout the
organisation as its successor New Johnston
is today.

London Transport and its predecessor
the Underground Group realised the value
of having a distinctive and unique typeface
for their enterprise. They recognised that
it was an important element of corporate
identity, as well as providing a clear and
precise letter form for basic communications
and display purposes. In the early years,
however, they never confused the importance
of clarity in communication with the need
to provide a corporate style. Pick seemingly
believed that a corporate style came from
the way things were done, not necessarily
from the tools used. During the 1920s and
'30s many typefaces were used to promote

the business, each of them appropriate to their particular use. The need dictated the style rather than the reverse.

New Johnston Typeface

London Transport continued to use the Johnston typeface in its various forms until the late 1970s, when it became clear that although this typeface in its original form retained a clarity and distinctiveness that was a valuable asset to the business, it was also extremely limited in its applications and fairly inflexible in use. Furthermore, it had been largely replaced on promotional material by other more adaptable faces. This is hardly surprising as the original face had been designed primarily for station names and display purposes. Although it was still used for in-house publications, external agencies found its limited range of well-worn display lettering too inhibiting and heavy-handed for advertising and promotional work.

In 1979 the designers and typographers Banks and Miles were asked by London Transport to look at the problem as part of a more general review of publicity, the assumption at the time being that Johnston would be dropped. Banks and Miles's recommendation was just the opposite, however: revive the face, develop a new range of fonts to provide flexibility and choice, and ensure that the 'new' fonts could be used for computer typesetting when this technology became available.

The objective was to develop a new range of typefaces that retained the distinctive character of Johnston, capitalised on its goodwill and eliminated the disadvantages inherent in a display-form lettering. The London Transport Board endorsed the proposed development and 'New Johnston' was designed in a range of fonts from bold to light including italics and condensed faces. It has since been adapted for computer typesetting and a new face called 'bookface' has been added. 'Bookface' is intended as a textface – a far cry from Johnston's original hand-drawn display lettering.

'New Johnston' (left), the amended typeface developed by Banks and Miles in the early 1980s which has a much broader range of applications beyond display lettering and can be computer typeset. The Night Buses booklet of 1987 (above) demonstrates its use on small format publicity material.

ABCDEFGHIJKLMN
OPQRSTUVWXYZab
cdefghijklmnopqrst
uvwxyz1234567890

One of the earliest pictorial posters, issued by the Underground in 1908. The artist, John Hassall, was also responsible for the famous railway travel poster showing a jolly fisherman running along the beach above the memorable slogan 'Skegness is so Bracing'.

Posters

By the late 1920s the Underground was being widely praised for its high standards of design in many areas, but particularly for the superb quality and variety of its pictorial posters. In 1927 the art critic of *The Times*, reviewing an exhibition, claimed that 'there can be no doubt at all that the credit for the earliest consistent use of good posters of any kind belongs to the Underground'. The origins of this reputation can be found nearly twenty years before in the early attempts by Frank Pick, as the Underground's first Traffic Officer, to encourage greater use of the company's newly opened tube lines. Pick was a lawyer and statistician by training, with no experience of marketing and publicity. With the poster he hit on the ideal way to promote the Underground Group's

new operations at a time when the company desperately needed to attract more passengers.

Pick seemed to sense instinctively the importance of style and image in promoting the company's product. From their original simple purpose of encouraging travel on the system, the posters grew into a distinctive and highly effective medium for promoting all aspects of the Underground and later London Transport. The visual images cultivated the notion that everything the great city had to offer was available through travel by bus, tram or Underground. It was a brilliant and very effective promotional concept. Pick had a passionate commitment to good design and an enlightened approach to the commercial application of art. The posters were commissioned for sound business reasons as a publicity exercise, but Pick believed that they

The sights and leisure
facilities of London
promoted by poster.
Three examples by Frank
Brangwyn, 1913 (top
left), Rex Whistler, 1928
(above) and Frank
Newbould, 1934 (left).

THERE IS STILL
THE COUNTRY

UNDERGROUND

KENWOOD

UNDERGROUND
to GOLDERS GREEN
or HIGHGATE STATION
thence by bus 210
to "The Spaniards"
Daily every 7½ minutes

TRAM
3, 5 to HAMPSTEAD
7, 15 to HIGHGATE Rd
11 to HIGHGATE VILLAGE
from Moorgate or Holborn
Daily every 5 minutes

By bus or Underground to London's countryside. Posters by Dora Batty, 1926 (above), Margaret Calkin James, 1935 (top right) and Roy Meldrum, 1933 (right). The Meldrum poster features the short-lived LPTB winged logo introduced in 1933, which was quickly abandoned in favour of a London Transport version of the existing Underground bar and circle device.

It's surprising what you see if you travel
GREEN LINE or GENERAL

also fulfilled a loftier purpose in enriching the quality of urban life in London.

Most of the early pictorial posters used before the First World War were the work of commercial artists employed by the printers. Pick soon moved beyond this limited source and made direct commissions to established artists like Frank Brangwyn, as well as experimenting with new and untried names. His greatest 'discovery' was the American-born Edward McKnight Kauffer, who produced his first Underground poster for Pick in 1915. Over the next twenty-five years Kauffer designed more than a hundred posters for the Underground and London Transport. He was undoubtedly the most original and innovative poster designer of his generation. Kauffer's influence on poster art was enormous, encouraging many radical new ideas in graphic design.

The 1920s and 1930s were a golden age of poster art in which the Underground and later London Transport led the field in this country. Pick rose to become Managing Director of the Underground in the 1920s and Vice Chairman of London Transport from 1933. Despite his much broader responsibilities he always maintained a close interest in the organisation's publicity, and the poster campaign was kept to the fore. London Transport became the leading patron of what was then called commercial art. For any aspiring young artist, a poster commission could be a tremendous career boost. The artwork would suddenly appear on hundreds of bus shelters and tube stations all over London – much better exposure than a small select show in a Bond Street gallery. A poster was also an attractive prospect for well-established artists, and there are few leading

A 1936 poster for the circus by Barnett Freedman, formed by posting two standard 'double royal' posters (each 40in. x 25in.) together to make a 'quad royal'.

names in the British art world between the wars who did not work at some time for London Transport.

When commissioned, an artist would usually be given a fairly broad brief. A title and subject for illustration would be suggested, with responsibility for lettering left to the printers. From the 1920s onwards the written message was usually set in the

BLACKBERRY SUNDAY by any GENERAL Bus

Above: A characteristic rural theme by Walter Spradbery, who designed more than eighty posters for the Underground and London Transport. This is a bus panel poster issued in 1929.

Right: 'Rugby at Twickenham' by Laura Knight, 1921.

RUGBY AT TWICKENHAM
BY TRAM
FROM HAMMERSMITH OR SHEPHERDS BUSH

Underground's own Johnston typeface, which has been used ever since as the clear and distinctive trademark of London Transport publicity. Artists were allowed considerable scope for self-expression in the pictorial content. Pick never imposed his own taste, which was fairly conservative, but judged each work on its 'fitness for purpose' – its effectiveness at conveying an idea or a message. 'There is room in posters for all styles,' he once commented. 'They are the most eclectic form of art. It is possible to move from the most literal representation to the wildest impressionism so long as the subject remains understandable to the man in the street.'

Unlike other advertisers who were competing with each other in the marketplace, London Transport had no direct competitors and could afford to take risks with its posters. Many of the artists commissioned were influenced by the avant-garde European art movements of the early twentieth century, and posters became a medium for popular commercial interpretation of these styles. Cubism, Futurism and Vorticism all reached the general public in Britain by the way of the Underground poster. The simplification of images into dramatic, geometrically based compositions – which was common to all these new art movements – was particularly appropriate to poster design. Alongside the 'modernist' graphics were a range of more traditional landscapes and 'realistic' representations of London and its countryside.

In nearly all of the posters the emphasis was on leisure pursuits. The commuter's custom might first be assured through an enticing view of a leafy suburb accessible with a cheap season ticket, but the real job of the posters was to encourage off-peak travel. They featured exhibitions, entertainment, sights, shopping or the simple delights of a walk in the country. Buses and

Left: Edward McKnight Kauffer's 'Winter Sales', 1921, a striking example of his avant-garde poster design. Here he has combined the influence of traditional Japanese woodcuts with the dynamic, swirling lines of Vorticist art, the British response to Cubism with which Kauffer was briefly associated.

Overleaf: A panel poster for the Oxford and Cambridge Boat Race by P. Drake Brookshaw, 1927. The graphic visual image makes mention of the event in the text redundant. This would have been posted on the glass draught screens inside Underground cars.

WiNTER SALES

are best reached by

UNDERGROUND

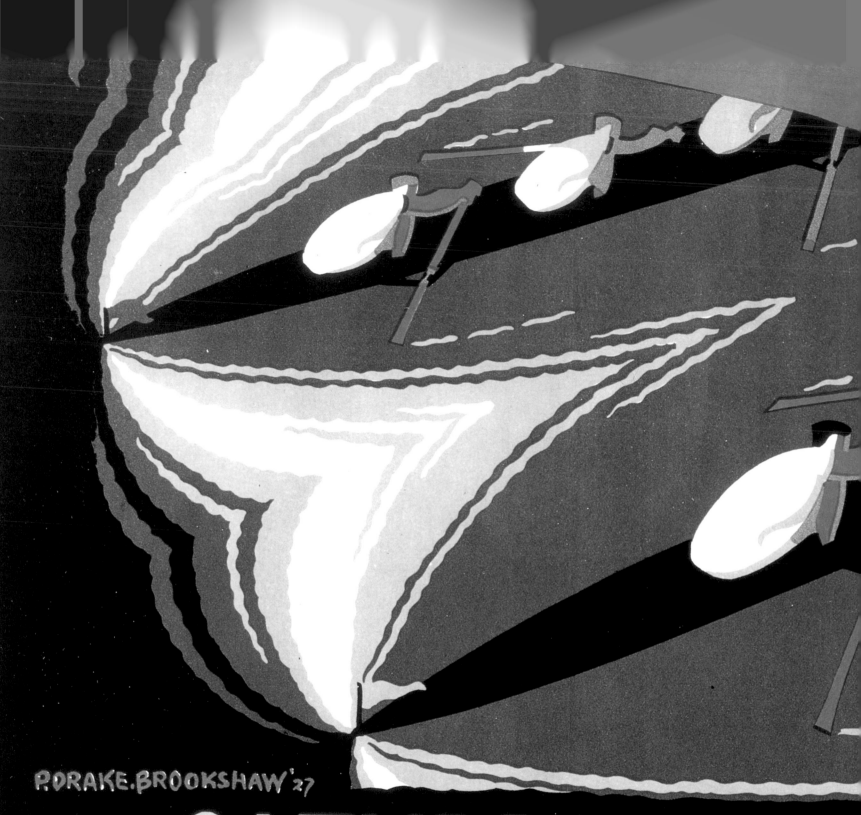

P.DRAKE.BROOKSHAW '27

SATURDAY MA

NEAREST STATIONS:- PUTNE

RAVENSCOURT PK, TURNH

RCH 31ST - 9·45 AM

Y BRIDGE, HAMMERSMITH

AM GREEN & CHISWICK PK

ROUND

Using modern art to sell season tickets. A poster by Jeffryes, 1929.

Left: The cover of a
London Transport
Pleasure Outings booklet,
featuring Green Line and
excursion services, 1936.

Below left: A London
County Council
Tramways poster by
John Farleigh, 1928.

trains rarely appeared: it was the destination,
not the experience of getting there that was
conjured up. These were artfully idealised
visions of the pleasures that could be had
through travelling on London Transport.

Before the creation of London Transport
in 1933, the London County Council
Tramways and the Metropolitan Railway,
the largest public transport operators in
London outside Pick's Underground Group,
both followed the Underground's lead in
poster publicity. The LCC produced a limited
number of large format posters for display
on tram shelters and in smaller sizes inside
trams, often using art students at the LCC
Central School of Arts and Crafts to design
them. Many of these are attractive images,
but the LCC posters never reached the range
and quality of the Underground's prodigious
output in the 1920s.

Right: Wartime women
workers bill posting early
Metro-land publicity for
the Metropolitan
Railway, c1916.

Below: Tempting city
workers with the rural
charms of 'London's
nearest countryside'.
The cover of a Metro-land
guide from the 1920s.

The Metropolitan produced a limited number of posters, but found a rather different promotional niche through its annual 'Metro-land' guides. Through a subsidiary, the company had cannily developed housing estates on surplus land near its stations in the areas north-west of London served by the line. 'Metro-land' was the catchy title given by the railway's publicity department to these areas in 1915. The annual Metro-land guidebook, a very high-quality production for its day on glossy paper with coloured plates, was the company's chosen publicity medium. Middle-class Londoners were encouraged to move out of town to new commuter homes in or close to the country but linked to the city by train. The message was reinforced by other promotional material in the form of postcards, calendars and country walks booklets: 'Metro-land, London's nearest countryside .... charm and peace await you. Those who visit it for the first time are enchanted by its beauty and never lose their love for it.'

The purple prose and romantic illustrations clearly worked, as both house building and season-ticket sales on the Metropolitan boomed in the 1920s. The Metro-land promotion ended in 1933 when London Transport took over, though publicity to entice Londoners out into the countryside by train continued. London Transport soon began publication of its long-running Country Walks series of booklets, pocket paperbacks with beautiful woodcut illustrations by Eric Ravilious. London Transport also broadened its range of publications to include general and specialist visitors' guides to London.

The Underground and
London Transport used
artworks and illustrations
in an astonishing variety
of styles. These three
humorous examples are
by Arnrid Johnston for
a press advertisement
of 1931 (right), Feliks
Topolski for a private
hire promotion in 1937
(below) and Fougasse for
a wartime information
poster of 1944 (bottom).

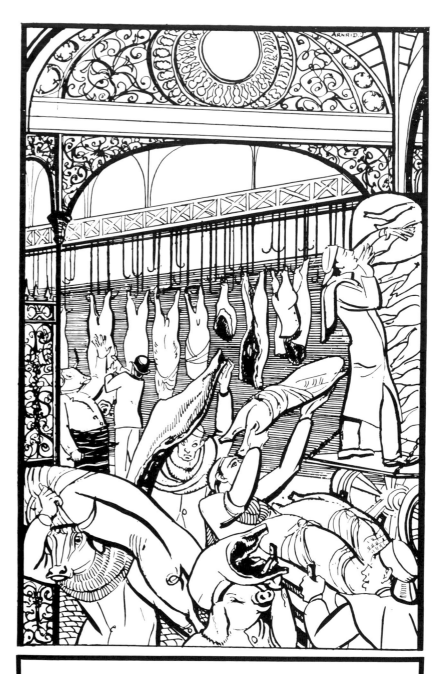

A BRITISH MARKET

SMITHFIELD MARKET—

BLACKFRIARS STATION

BUY! BUY!—BY

E 3 '992/31

BRIGHTEST LONDON
IS BEST REACHED BY
UNDERGROUND

Both the Underground and London Transport advertised almost daily in the national and local London press between the wars, sometimes with a carefully crafted written message only, but often using graphic illustrations by some of the best commercial artists and book illustrators of the time, including Clare Leighton, Edward Bawden and Feliks Topolski. The insistence on high standards of production, even for something as ephemeral as a single press advertisement, was always there, and was applied equally in the publication of other promotional material ranging from timetables and guides explaining how the system worked, to children's story books and toy theatre designs. An Underground or London Transport publication always had the hallmarks of quality and thoughtful presentation.

The Second World War effectively halted London Transport's publicity work and saw Frank Pick's departure to the Ministry of Information in 1940. The posters, reduced in size and quantity because of wartime paper shortages, took on the new role of morale boosting both for passengers and staff in the dark days of the Blitz and the blackout. After the war, London Transport was carrying more passengers than ever before and no longer needed to encourage greater use of the system. The Pick tradition of pictorial posters was nevertheless revived by the new Publicity Officer, Harold Hutchison. His principal innovation was the pair poster, an arrangement whereby one poster was devoted entirely to artwork, with a second alongside

Above: Cover of a Country Walks booklet with woodcut illustration by Eric Ravilious, 1938. London Transport continued to publish its popular Country Walks series until 1980.

Above left: The smart way to travel. A poster by Horace Taylor, 1924.

Left: Underground press advertisement illustrated by Edward Bawden, 1928.

THE THEATRE

THERE are 39 Theatres in Central London, and every one of them is within easy reach of one or more Underground Stations. They offer 41,000 seats for the choice. There are special trains in service for the convenience of Theatre-goers, running in non-stop from the outer terminals. After the performance there is no need to risk the comedy of taxi-hunting; the drama of finding your car; or the tragedy of catching a cold. For most of the last homeward trains leave the central stations at 12.30 a.m. Every one deserves a night out once a week. Let every one see that he gets it. You will ring down the curtain on a happy evening if you travel home by

U N D E R G R O U N D

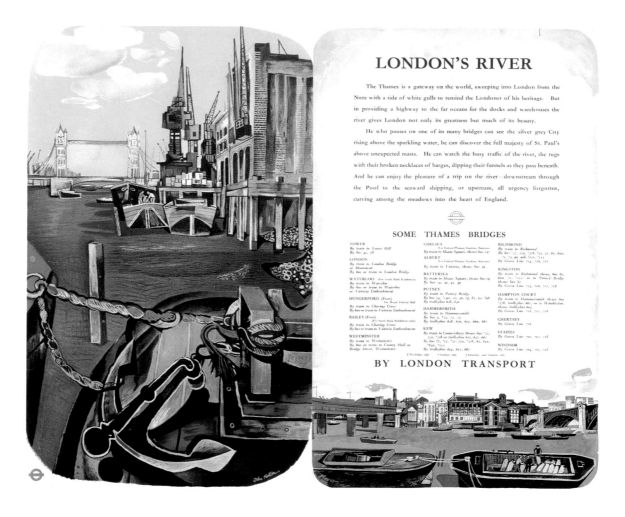

LONDON'S RIVER

The Thames is a gateway on the world, sweeping into London from the Nore with a tide of white gulls to remind the Londoner of his heritage. But in providing a highway to the far oceans for the docks and warehouses the river gives London not only its greatness but much of its beauty.

He who pauses on one of its many bridges can see the silver grey City rising above the sparkling water, he can discover the full majesty of St. Paul's above unexpected masts. He can watch the busy traffic of the river, the tugs with their broken necklaces of barges, dipping their funnels as they pass beneath. And he can enjoy the pleasure of a trip on the river—downstream through the Pool to the seaward shipping, or upstream, all urgency forgotten, curving among the meadows into the heart of England.

SOME THAMES BRIDGES

BY LONDON TRANSPORT

A pair poster by John Minton, 1951. This layout allowed greater freedom of expression to both artist and copywriter.

carrying text for information. This allowed the artist greater freedom of expression as well as providing London Transport's copywriters with more space in which to expand on their subject. The idea was to attract the viewer with a large, uncluttered artwork and then offer extensive travel and other information for anyone who was waiting for a train or a bus.

Compared with the pre-war years, the posters issued from the 1950s onwards are disappointing and seem limited in range. This reflected an apparent shortage of talented young graphic artists, but it also suggests an unadventurous commissioning policy by Pick's successors. The arrival of television advertising and new colour magazines as promotional media also undermined the role of the poster as a publicity tool. In the 1960s and 1970s London

Transport battled with a succession of problems: financial difficulties, staff shortages, service unreliability and a decline in passenger numbers. Art poster publicity did not appear to offer any solutions to these setbacks and became widely regarded as an irrelevant luxury that the organisation could no longer afford. At the height of the art poster campaign in the 1920s the Underground had issued a new design almost every week; by the late 1970s this had fallen to no more than one or two direct commissions to artists each year. Most advertising work for London Transport was now contracted out to agencies who tended to use photographic images rather than artworks for posters. There were occasional flashes of inspiration such as the award-winning 'Fly the Tube' poster of 1977 promoting the new Piccadilly Line extension to Heathrow. On the whole, however, output

A pair poster by Denys
Nichols displayed at
Dollis Hill station, 1950.
The integrated concrete
unit combining the
station nameboard, poster
display and lighting is a
Holden design from the
late 1930s.

Paint the town by Tube
Convenient stations: Leicester Square, Piccadilly Circus

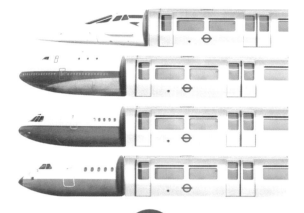

Fly the Tube

Take the Piccadilly Line to Heathrow Airport.
It's the only way to fly.

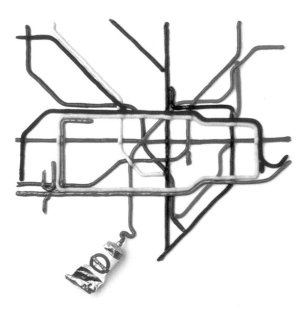

Above: Rather belatedly, London Underground began commissioning innovative graphic design again in the 1980s. This poster by Su Huntley and Donna Muir first appeared as an escalator panel in 1987.

Top right: The award-winning 'Fly the Tube' poster by Geoff Senior of FCB Advertising, 1977, a clever design from an otherwise uninspired period of publicity work by the main outside agency used by London Transport.

Right: 'Tate Gallery' by David Booth of The Fine White Line Design, 1986, has proved the most popular of the 'Art on the Underground' posters and has been sold in large numbers through the London Transport Museum shop.

THE TATE GALLERY
by Tube

Dancing in the street

Enjoy open-air London by Tube

Carnival by Paula Cox
A new work of art commissioned by London Underground

Art on the Underground   © London Underground Limited

was dull and it rarely matched the innovation and variety of previous campaigns.

Happily, London Transport's dwindling reputation as a patron of the arts was successfully revived in the 1980s as part of a new marketing initiative. 'Art on the Underground' is neither an advertising nor a publicity scheme. It is a form of corporate art sponsorship whereby London Underground commissions half a dozen new works of art each year and reproduces them as posters. The subjects are loosely connected with the Underground as potential destinations but they are not intended primarily as travel promotions. Although not always successful as posters, they are an attractive and cost-effective means of improving and regularly changing the appearance of the Underground for passengers. They brighten the whole of the Underground and successfully complement station modernisation, which can only be achieved on a long timescale and with considerable capital investment. The method may differ somewhat from Frank Pick's approach over fifty years ago, but the ultimate intention is much the same. Art has again become an integral part of London Transport's corporate objectives in providing millions of Londoners and visitors with a pleasant environment for travel.

Above left: Using art to improve the environment of the Underground. The 1930s platforms at Knightsbridge were refurbished in the 1980s and are seen here with large format posters of newly commissioned artworks by Julian Trevelyan and John Bellany (far right) in 1988.

Above: 'Dancing in the Street' by Paula Cox, issued just before the Notting Hill Carnival in August 1994.

Environments such as stations or bus shelters can colour passengers' perception of a transport service. London Transport inherited from its various constituent companies a large and diverse stock of

buildings and environments, ranging from the Holden brick drums to the small suburban stations of the Metropolitan Railway. Frank Pick was the first to recognise the importance of providing a pleasant environment for waiting passengers. He also realised that the diverse buildings could be presented as a cohesive network by imposing on them common standards of signage, identity and hardware. Very little has changed today. There are an amazing variety of stations and other buildings, many altered or rebuilt several times, and amongst them representatives of almost every architectural style of the last 130 years, yet they are all recognisably part of London Transport's infrastructure.

The First Underground Railway

The first section of the Metropolitan Railway, between Bishop's Road, Paddington, and Farringdon Street, was opened on 10 January 1863. It was the first urban underground railway in the world, so it is perhaps not surprising that contemporary newspapers and journals gave more column inches to the remarkable engineering achievements than to the architecture of the seven original stations on the line. Nevertheless, *The Times* reported, with some exaggeration, that 'the King's Cross Station is as large, as lofty and as well lighted as any of the great Metropolitan Termini'.

All the stations were designed by John Fowler, the company's Chief Engineer, and had single-storey buildings at street level in an Italianate style. They were brick built, with imitation stone facing and decoration in a Portland cement described as 'Ransom's Patent Stone'. Only three of the original stations, those built directly below the Marylebone and Euston Roads at Baker Street, Portland Road (now Great Portland Street) and Gower Street (now Euston Square), were actually underground at platform level. Construction was not by tunnelling underground but by 'cut and cover'. This meant digging a trench, supporting the side walls with brick, roofing over the track bed and reinstating the road surface above at ground level. The other four stations were given high iron and glass train sheds supported by the brick retaining walls on each side of the railway cutting. The wooden station platforms were illuminated by gas lamps in large glass bowls suspended from the roof.

The Metropolitan District Railway, which began running its first services between South Kensington and Westminster Bridge in 1868, was a separate company from the Metropolitan, but Fowler again acted as Chief Engineer and was responsible for most of its early station designs. Once the two railways had been linked at both ends to form the Inner Circle (now the Circle Line) in 1884 there was little to distinguish their respective

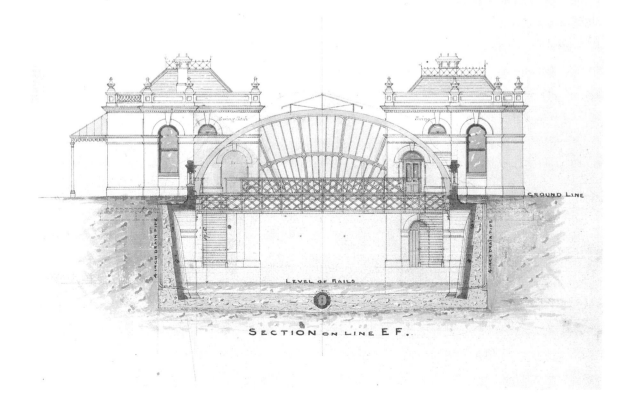

SECTION on LINE E F.

stations on the line. Bayswater and West Brompton are the only two that have retained their original street-level buildings largely untouched.

Both the Metropolitan and the District were extended rapidly into and beyond the western and north-western suburbs. There the District chose a variant on the sedate Italianate style favoured by many of the main-line railway companies for suburban and branch-line stations. The Metropolitan Extension Line to Harrow featured some quaint cottage-style architecture from Finchley Road onwards, approvingly described by *Harper's*

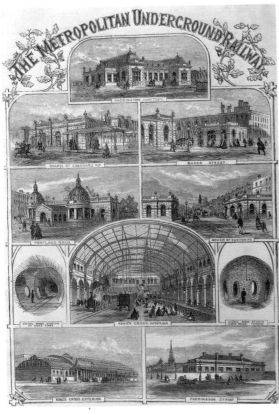

Monthly Magazine in 1884 as 'a modest adaptation of "Old Kensington" to the most practical purpose'.

When the District and the inner section of the Metropolitan were electrified in 1905 both companies began to rebuild many of their original stations, this time employing professional architects. Harry W. Ford provided the District Railway with a series of new designs which he varied according to the surroundings of the station. At Temple, for example, which was rebuilt in 1915, the style of the new station on the Embankment with its Portland stone façade was chosen to blend with the arches and balustrading of nearby Somerset House. At less sensitive sites, Ford often used golden-brown glazed terracotta for the main street façade, best seen today at Fulham Broadway, Barons Court and Earls Court which were all completed in 1905–11.

Above left: Watercolour of Temple station, 1915, by architect Harry W. Ford. The Portland stone façade was designed to blend with nearby Somerset House.

Left: The seven original stations of the Metropolitan Railway, all designed by John Fowler. These views were published by the *Illustrated London News* on 27 December 1862, just before the line opened.

Glazed terracotta façade
to Fulham Broadway
station, rebuilt in 1910–11
by Harry W. Ford.
Illustration by Neil
Gower, 1994.

The District had by this time become part of Yerkes' Underground Group and its station upgrading reflected the company's wish to give its recently electrified acquisition an image which matched its three new tube railways. The tubes required a new approach to station design because they mostly occupied small, awkward surface sites within an

existing built-up street, and they needed a new layout to accommodate the lifts. The first deep-level underground line, the City and South London, employed architect T. Phillips Figgis to design its station buildings. These were modest single-storey booking halls in a red brick Italianate style, their most distinguishing feature being a large dome and cupola which housed the lift mechanism. Kennington is the only station which still retains this feature. Despite the remarkable innovation of electric underground trains, the line used gas lamps in the stations to supplement the meagre electric lighting, and access to the platforms was by hydraulic lift. Full electrification of these services did not come until the line was extended at both ends between 1900 and 1907, when the power supply was upgraded.

The Central London Railway (now the Central Line), opened between Shepherds Bush and the Bank in 1900, was a more ambitious project from the start. The stations on the 'Twopenny Tube', as it was known, had most of the features now familiar to London Underground travellers – electric lifts and lighting, tiled platform tunnels, and street-level booking halls designed to have offices built above them. The standardised station entrances, designed by Harry B. Measures, were described in the railway's publicity material as being stylistically 'a kind of Renaissance carried out in terracotta'. In fact the style is so unassuming that the buildings barely register as underground stations and their 'street presence' is minimal. The best preserved example of an original Twopenny Tube station is Holland Park.

The common management of the three Underground Group tubes, the Bakerloo, Piccadilly and Hampstead (Northern) lines, meant that station design was standardised along with rolling stock, signalling and other equipment. Yerkes employed the young architect Leslie Green to design stations which were distinctive and conspicuous by both day and night. They remain instantly recognisable today by their characteristic exterior finish of glazed dark red bricks. The glaze made them easy to clean and the unusual colour certainly stood out in the street by day, although it would have looked almost black under the original arc lights at night.

As the lift machinery had to be at first-floor level, two-storey surface buildings were necessary, with load-bearing steel-frame construction to allow the addition of lettable office storeys above the booking hall. The terracotta cladding was chosen because it allowed various decorative mouldings to be turned out quickly and cheaply. Three contractors were asked to erect samples at Lillie Bridge depot, each consisting of two piers supporting an arch. Stanley Heaps, who was Green's assistant at the time and later succeeded him as the Underground's architect, recalled that the familiar design of the station façades, and the colour, were chosen on this basis; it was a mass-produced

and virtually off-the-peg system. According to Heaps 'the price was at a flat rate of ten shillings per foot of the elevation, openings deducted'. The chosen contractors who supplied and installed the glazed bricks, which went under the trade name of Burmantofts Faience, were the Leeds Fireclay Company.

Leslie Green also designed the decorative schemes for the booking hall interiors, passageways and platforms which were all part tiled, with art nouveau-style grilles and doors on the lifts. Station names were picked out in tiles at either end of each platform, with bands and patterns of white and coloured

Opposite (top): Stockwell station by T. Phillips Figgis photographed on the opening day of the City and South London Railway, the first tube, 4 November 1890.

Opposite (bottom): Central London Railway station at Notting Hill Gate by Harry B. Measures, 1900. The station entrances are inconspicuous but the big TUBE sign indicates clearly, if brashly, what the little decorative terracotta building concealed. The air space above the station is to let.

Left: Piccadilly Tube platform by Leslie Green, 1906, showing colour coding in bands of tiles and the original station name system. From a coloured postcard of the period.

Below left: A watercolour of Green's design for Oxford Circus station exhibited at the Royal Academy in 1905.

Above: Typical Leslie Green booking hall with decorative tiled ticket window at Covent Garden station, 1907, photographed in 1921.

Right: Tiled original Way Out sign of 1906 still *in situ* at Gloucester Road station. Features such as this are now preserved and restored wherever possible.

Opposite: Covent Garden station by Leslie Green, 1907. Drawing by David Gentleman, 1994.

tiling throughout. 'A different colour is used for each station, so that habitual passengers on the railway will speedily be able to tell what station they are at without having to look at the name' explained *The Tramway and Railway World*, reporting on construction progress in 1905. The magazine made the further observation that 'On an ordinary open air railway, the regular traveller recognises stations by their appearance and surroundings, but as there is no aid of this kind on a tube railway, the plan of using different colours for the names and decorations has been adopted, and it ought to prove very useful'. In practice, it was decided after only a few years' operation to augment the visual colour-coding of each station and the limited signage with an early version of the roundel nameplate fixed at intervals along each platform. This had the station name in white on a blue bar across a solid red enamel disc, a design first introduced on the District Railway in about 1908 and later extended to the Underground Group's three tubes. The continuous frieze with the station name all along the platform wall was not introduced until the 1930s.

More than thirty of the Leslie Green stations were opened on the three Underground Group tube lines in 1906–7, a remarkable exercise in mass production. The pressure to get so much done in so short a time may well have affected the architect's health as Green died in 1908 aged only 33. He was succeeded by his assistant Stanley Heaps who remained the Underground Group's, and subsequently London Transport's, architect until he retired in 1943. Heaps' early work included the stations on the first Bakerloo Line extension opened in 1915, where the designs are an attractive development of Green's original standard layouts, amended partly in order to incorporate escalators instead of lifts. Maida Vale and Kilburn Park, the only two with surface buildings, remain the most attractive of all the early tube stations.

Above: Mosaic roundel at Maida Vale, 1915.

Top and right: Kilburn Park booking hall, 1915, by Stanley Heaps, recently renovated by London Underground.

The stations designed by Heaps for the Bakerloo Line extension were an attractive development of the Leslie Green style. Maida Vale and Kilburn Park are particularly good examples.

The Suburban Stations

The first major extension to the Underground system after the First World War was the projection of the Hampstead Tube in 1923–4, nearly five miles north of Golders Green to Edgware. The five new stations have neo-Georgian booking halls fronted by Doric colonnades in Portland stone. It is a cosy style which looked appropriate both in the original semi-rural settings of the stations and in the sea of suburban development which subsequently engulfed them. By the 1930s the new line had transformed Edgware from a tiny village into a substantial commuter suburb, and the open land around Burnt Oak station was covered by the London County Council's largest north London housing estate.

Heaps explained the decision to adopt an architectural style quite different from the inner London tube stations in a talk he gave in 1927:

> The call for buildings that blatantly advertised the railway was not so strong, partly because the railway here was above ground and advertised itself. As the line traversed a dormitory district it was thought that station architecture having a touch of domestic feeling about it would be in harmony with the environment. The stations of the Edgware Line were sufficiently dignified to command respect, and sufficiently pleasing to promote affection – it helped the daily round of life if the first step in the morning inspired pleasant thoughts!

Whether the line's regular users appreciated this concern for their well-being is not recorded, but the stations have worn well in the last seventy years.

Frank Pick had by this time risen to become Assistant Managing Director of the Underground Group and had broadened his design interests in the company well beyond his original publicity brief to include architecture and engineering. Although the Edgware Line stations were adequate for the task, Pick was not entirely satisfied with them and looked outside the company in a search for what he called a new architectural idiom.

The architect chosen for this experiment was Charles Holden, whose work had been rather undistinguished in the arts and crafts manner but who was clearly seeking an opportunity to be more adventurous. He and Pick had first met in 1915 at the inaugural meeting of the Design and Industries Association. Holden's first commission from the Underground was to design the small back entrance to Westminster station. The result was a simple but confident construction showing the beginnings of a style that was developed and refined in his later work on the Morden extension. Holden had obviously passed his first test because Pick then commissioned him to modernise a group of stations on the southern part of the City and South London (now the Northern Line). The work was largely confined to upgrading and modernising booking halls and façades. His

Above: Untitled poster by Fred Taylor, 1925, showing suburban development around a gleaming new tube station. The Hampstead Tube was extended overground from Golders Green to Edgware in 1923/4. The station depicted, fronted by a Doric colonnade, is typical of the Edgware Line designs by Stanley Heaps.

Below: The forecourt at
Heaps' Edgware terminus
in 1926, two years after
completion, when it was
already a busy suburban
station.

approach was to rationalise the often chaotic layout of the interior and to provide a more modern façade that was designed to stand out in the suburban street. Oval, with its unadorned pediment and simple façade, is clearly a development of his work at Westminster. As one would expect from alteration rather than new building, the design of these stations is not entirely

Below: The forecourt at Heaps' Edgware terminus in 1926, two years after completion, when it was already a busy suburban station.

successful, but Holden was clearly developing design ideas.

This commission was followed by another to design all the new stations on the extension south of Clapham Common to Morden which opened in 1926. There for the first time Holden could develop his ideas properly. The new stations were nearly all to be built on corner sites, but each one was slightly different in size and plan. Holden's response was to devise a series of folding screen façades in Portland stone. This was an ingenious idea as the angle of the façades could be altered to suit the particular conditions of each site. At the same time, a consistent image was maintained in a variety of suburban settings. Since such a radical change in station identity was being proposed, the ideas were tried out first in model form. In 1925 a full-size mock up was constructed in one of the former

exhibition buildings at Earls Court, and for some months Holden and Pick changed details until they were satisfied that their plan would work. In essence it was an extremely simple idea and could have been boring in execution, but Holden gave each station a sense of drama and importance. With their lack of unnecessary ornamentation and flat stone façades, these buildings appeared strikingly modern in their largely Victorian suburban setting. When the new line first opened there was even a searchlight on the roof of each building to draw attention to the station and reinforce its visual impact.

It was with this group of stations that Holden developed his ideas on light. Each of the façades contains a large window with a stained-glass roundel, which allows natural light into the booking hall during the day; interior lighting illuminates the roundel at night. The image of the company was thus projected within a simple architectural framework in a way that was both bold and imaginative. Pick was particularly keen to ensure that the roundel was properly illuminated, noting that 'some slight modification in the lighting is also necessary on the outside to ensure that the bull's-eye signs fixed on the canopy are illuminated over the whole extent of their surface'. This was done by adding external floodlights. He was also greatly concerned that allowance should be made for later poster additions to the façade, so that they could be accommodated within the design. His attention to detail was already beginning to be felt on the architecture, as it had been with publicity.

It is perhaps disappointing that the treatment of the spaces below ground, which did not involve Holden, is less radical, relying on a more decorative approach with bands of coloured tiles. But on the whole, Pick was pleased with the Morden Line work. In the brochure produced for the opening in September 1926 he wrote:

Left: Charles Holden's first major commission for new stations was for the southern extension to the City and South London Line. In order to test his ideas a mock up was constructed in a redundant exhibition building at Earls Court. This remained there for several months whilst Holden and Pick refined the details.

Bottom: Tooting Bec station by Charles Holden, 1926, showing the 'folding screen' principle in operation. Particularly interesting are the large glazed screen fronts incorporating the roundel – and the witty three-dimensional roundel capitals. These photographs show the recent renovation of this station which included the installation of replica roundel masts with the original UNDERGROUND lettering style.

The design is of no particular school; it neither apes the past nor underlines modernity by violating taste. It is an attempt to show the purpose of the building in a manner combining simplicity and strength with grace and character. ... the public should have no difficulty in recognising an underground station.

Although Pick had a consuming passion for architecture and design, he was above all a commercial manager and judged things according to their contribution to the business. Recognition of a building as a station was the first test of its success. The folding screen idea was used again on later rebuilt stations such as Leicester Square and Knightsbridge, although none succeeded as well as the original.

The 'folding screen' presented as a flat front at Morden, photographed in 1934, eight years after completion. All the suburban housing beyond the station had been built in the interim, and a network of feeder bus services extended the station's catchment area even further.

Right: Bank, 1926. The first of the sub-surface ticket halls with several street exits. Its grim functionalism is in stark contrast to Holden's Piccadilly Circus of 1928 (above), where every element down to the waste bins had been designed to create an attractive and inviting environment. This contemporary artist's impression is by Cyril Farey.

Holden's Prestige Projects

Two other major projects attracted considerable attention at the time: Piccadilly Circus, which by the late 1920s was unable to cope with the passenger throughput, and had to be completely rebuilt and enlarged; and 55 Broadway, the new Headquarters of the Underground Group.

When Piccadilly Circus station was opened in 1906 it dealt with about 1.5 million passengers a year. By the early 1920s this figure had grown to over 20 million, and was increasing every year. There was little scope for enlarging the surface buildings, so it was decided to excavate a new ticket hall underneath the road junction. An almost circular plan effectively reproduced below ground the layout of John Nash's original 1820s circus which a century later had been nearly obliterated by redevelopment and was certainly no longer circus-shaped.

A sub-surface booking hall with a series of street exits had first been tried out with the reconstruction of Bank station in 1925–6. This was functional but grim. Holden's contribution at Piccadilly Circus was to turn the engineers' bleak hole in the ground into an attractive environment. In the centre were new escalators, which replaced the original lifts, and banks of automatic ticket machines. Around these was what Holden called the 'ambulatory', a walkway with a curved arcade of display windows and lamps hanging from ceiling columns. The intended effect was that of a shopping street at night, and some of the display windows were used by the retailers above ground such as Swan and Edgar.

The ticket hall was finely detailed with specially designed lights, litter bins and information panels. High-quality materials were used for all finishes including Travertine marble cladding and bronze fittings. The design was an immediate success when it opened in 1928 and was repeated elsewhere, but never on such a scale or so lavishly. This was very much a prestige project for the Underground, and to underline Piccadilly's position at the heart of London and, by extension, London's prominence as a leading world city, a special large map of the world was installed which displayed the time at other points on the globe. The artist Stephen Bone was also commissioned to design a giant illustrated map of the world which homed in on London. This was displayed with large artworks showing the objectives of Underground travel – business, shopping and entertainment – on panels above and beside the escalators to be viewed as the passenger descended. Pick, ever the commercial manager, had these replaced within a few years by a giant Ovaltine advertisement, much to Holden's annoyance.

Piccadilly Circus was acclaimed internationally as the most advanced metro environment anywhere in the world. It made a particularly strong impression on one of the Soviet engineers planning the new Moscow Metro in the early 1930s. Nikita Krushchev,

Left: Stephen Bone (left) at work on his mural for Piccadilly Circus station, 1928, depicting London as the hub of the world. Shortly afterwards Bone was married to the artist Mary Adshead, who also produced artworks for the Underground. She recalls that the fee for his Piccadilly work paid for their honeymoon.

who had become responsible for the Metro project as the Second Secretary of the Moscow City Party Committee, recalled in his memoirs how the young engineer persuaded Stalin and himself to follow the London Underground's methods: 'He kept citing England as an example: Piccadilly Station in London, right in the heart of the most aristocratic section of the city, was built deep in the ground and it had escalators rather than elevators'. As a result the communists decided to take capitalist advice. London Underground was asked to undertake a full consultancy report on the Moscow Metro, and when the first line opened in 1935 it incorporated many features of the London system including escalators with column uplighters in the Holden mould. Architecturally, the Russians soon went far beyond Holden's decorative style to create palatial marble halls underground, but the consultancy had another long-term spin-off for London Transport. Requests for planning assistance soon came from other cities building metros around the world who turned to London for advice, and out of this came London Transport International, the overseas consultancy section of the business.

The other major project of the 1920s was the Headquarters of the Underground Group. This was constructed above St James's Park Station in 1927–9, and was at that time the

largest office building in London. Built on a corner site in a cruciform shape which allows light into all parts of the building, it is stepped back from a two-storey podium in five stages to a tower; its bulk is thus cleverly concealed. Pick was preoccupied with ensuring that the station under the building had sufficient street presence, and easy access from both sides. The solution was a passage cut through the building with an entrance to the ticket hall from each side. Holden achieved simplicity and grandeur in this building, without resorting to the usual application of assorted classical add-ons favoured by most architects of office buildings at that time.

The building was awarded the Royal Institute of British Architects' London Architectural Medal of 1929, but it also gained some public notoriety at the time because of the sculptures decorating it. The eight on the upper storeys, representing the four winds, include works by Eric Gill and Henry Moore. These attracted less attention than the two large sculptures called *Night* and *Day* which were carved in situ by Jacob Epstein at first-floor level. The figures were heavily criticised in the popular press and by some art critics as primitive, ugly and indecent. One was even attacked by vandals who threw paint over it. The controversy was such that Pick, feeling that he should back his architect's judgement on this despite his own dislike of Epstein's work, tendered his resignation. It was not accepted. The sculptures stayed, although as a deliberately absurd gesture of compromise Epstein chipped an inch off the penis of the naked young boy depicted in *Day*.

The building was carefully cleaned in 1986 and can be seen properly again now that the soot and grime of more than fifty years has been removed. 55 Broadway and its sculptures no longer attract special attention, but its fine design remains a supreme example of how to integrate an underground station

Right: 55 Broadway by night, the Headquarters of the Underground Group and later London Transport by Charles Holden, 1927–9. At the time of its construction, it was the largest office building in London.

Above and left:
The sculptures on
55 Broadway created
a considerable amount
of attention in their day.
The most contentious
were Jacob Epstein's
Day (left, after recent
cleaning) and *Night*
(right, being carved *in situ*
by the sculptor c1928).

Above: Chiltern Court
by Charles Clark, the
block of flats built over
Baker Street station in
the 1920s. The building
was less successful than
55 Broadway at
integrating commercial
development and public
transport.

Right: Willesden Green
station, Metropolitan
Railway, rebuilt by
Charles Clark in 1925.

into an office development and give each equal prominence and dignity. In this respect it is an interesting contrast to Chiltern Court, the huge block of luxury flats built by the Metropolitan Railway over its most important interchange station, Baker Street, which was completed at much the same time. Charles Clark's design for the Metropolitan has a certain pompous grandeur, and was then the largest apartment building in London, but now that the canopy is gone there is no real indication that this enormous pile conceals an underground station. Ensuring that every station was visible in the street, with clear and unambiguous signage, was an essential matter which – unlike their contemporaries working for other railways, and indeed their successors at London Transport – Pick and his architect understood very well.

Clark had provided the Metropolitan with some much more successful and less pretentious new station designs in the 1920s and early 1930s before its merger with the Underground to form London Transport. He was a competent company architect in the same mould as Heaps, but lacked Holden's inventiveness and sparkle. Many of the Metropolitan's urban stations were rebuilt at street level in this period with distinctive white-tiled façades and booking-hall interiors with nicely detailed mosaic decoration on the walls. Farringdon, Paddington, Great Portland Street, Edgware Road and Willesden Green are good examples of this treatment. Out in the suburbs where the Metropolitan opened two new branches to Watford (1925) and Stanmore (1932), Clark devised a quite different cottage-style station building with deep-pitched roofs that matched the new semi-detached houses and shopping parades of Metro-land.

The next big tranche of work undertaken by Holden for the Underground was a radical alternative to Clark's approach and defined the new house style that London Transport

was to maintain after 1933. The stations were both new and rebuilt designs for the extension of the Piccadilly Line to the north and west. In most cases the surface sites allowed more scope for experiment than the tightly constrained urban street corners of the Morden Line. Holden could have followed the fairly conservative example of Clark in Metro-land, or indeed of Heaps with his neo-Georgian stations on the Edgware line, but he chose to break with tradition completely. He also decided to work with brick and concrete as his main materials rather than Portland stone.

Both the form and materials of the new Piccadilly Line stations owe much to a visit that Pick and Holden made to Northern Europe and Scandinavia in the Summer of 1930. The purpose of the visit was to extend their knowledge of modern architecture, and it is clear that what they saw, particularly the work of the Dutch architect Willem Dudok in Hilversum, had a great influence on Holden's future work. Dudok's civic buildings

Above: Ladies Room sign in mosaic at Farringdon station, rebuilt by Clark in 1922–3. This attractive detail was a victim of refurbishment in the 1980s.

Left: The City Hall at Hilversum, Holland, by Willem Dudok, 1928–30. Dudok's work was greatly admired by Pick and Holden on their European tour of 1930.

Below right: Two views of Sudbury Town by Charles Holden, 1931. The first of the radically new 'brick box' stations designed for the Piccadilly Line, Sudbury Town heralded a new era in Underground architecture.

Below: Holden designed many of the products that were associated with the architecture. These simple globe lights at Sudbury Town were particularly successful.

combined an austere modern classicism with a simple industrial tradition, well suited to railway architecture.

The first of the new stations built in this 'European' style was Sudbury Town in the western suburbs. Completed in 1931, it is, as Holden himself described it, 'a brick box with a concrete lid'. If that sounds uninspiring,

the reality is far from it. The box is double height, with four large windows arranged symmetrically above the entrance, rising to the name frieze below the cornice. The arrangement of the station was conceived to promote the most efficient movement of people, a generously spaced ticket hall at the main entrance with direct access to one platform, and a covered concrete bridge to the other. A second, more modest entrance is provided on the other side of the tracks.

Sudbury Town represented an extraordinary leap forward in station design in this country, and heralded a new era in Underground architecture. What Holden had achieved was a simple, elegant structure using basic materials in an honest way. This combination could and would be developed and used many times over in slightly different ways. The same design elements were carried

through on to the platforms, with concrete canopies, glazed waiting areas, and even precast concrete fences. Particularly good was a Bauhaus-style platform lamp designed by Holden, a globe fitting held in a metal ring and used on top of a concrete post. This lamp was one of Holden's most successful designs and was used many times on the

Underground system. All this contrasted with some of the interior elements that Holden did not design, however. Pick was delighted with the station but dismayed that there were discordant additions, and issued an instruction that in future Holden was to be responsible for all elements of design within stations. Pick was particularly annoyed to find that much of the station hardware had been added without thought for its effect on the total environment:

On the platforms I found that some seven or eight automatic machines have been dumped down and are now going to spoil the cleanness and clearness of the platforms. Somehow there seems to be a desire on the part of everyone to break up and destroy the tidiness and spaciousness of this station. The only way in which, in my opinion, the spaciousness can be filled properly is by passengers, and not by a lot of impediments.

This would find many echoes amongst today's designers and architects who sometimes despair at what happens when they finish their work. Pick's concern was not that there should be no commercial activities, but that they should be considered at the design stage and integrated seamlessly into the whole. Thereafter he asked the Operating Manager to provide Holden with a complete list of all fittings and equipment that would be needed in each new station, and Holden was given final responsibility for ensuring that all these items were incorporated in the design from the start. Holden either designed or selected everything from seats and ticket machines to clocks and litter bins, and determined the final position of all these items.

Sudbury Town was followed by Sudbury Hill, Alperton and Acton Town; all using similar materials and following a similar form with variations. At Sudbury Hill and Acton Town, Holden created a canopy, making the entrance less austere, and providing greater opportunities to incorporate other elements such as shops. Whenever possible, Holden took great care to incorporate retailing into a station; in the Piccadilly Line stations he used the shop units to extend the façades and improve the line of the building. The combination of station and retailing was employed successfully at Turnpike Lane, Southgate and Rayners Lane. Turnpike Lane

Left: Turnpike Lane station by Holden, 1932. The double-height ticket hall is lit by clerestory windows giving a feeling of light and space to the interior.

Above: Arnos Grove by Holden, 1932. The similarity to Eric Asplund's drum-shaped Stockholm City Library of 1928 (right) can clearly be seen.

Far right: Boston Manor station tower by Holden, 1933.

worked particularly well since it was also a bus and tram terminus and occupied a site with a large street frontage. Holden used the frontage for shops as a continuation of the street, putting the vehicle turning and waiting areas at the back, rather than at the front as in so many stations.

In addition to the square box theme Holden experimented with other forms: the circular or semicircular drum shape, notably at Arnos Grove and Chiswick Park, and the tower and beacon stations as at Osterley and Boston Manor. Arnos Grove is the most successful of the drum stations. It is really a

The Boston Manor tower is a thin brick slab and has a top section of transparent glass which is illuminated at night. The glass section bisects part of the tower so that when lit it draws the eye down to the entrance. This is a particularly effective device, and it is rather surprising that it was not used again.

Below left: Southgate, 1933, the most unusual of Holden's stations. The low circular form is shown to best effect at night.

circular version of Acton Town or Sudbury Hill, in that it uses the same proportions and the projecting canopy idea. Unlike Chiswick Park, it does not have the rather incongruous brick tower to one side unbalancing the design. The drum style appears to have been particularly influenced by new north European architecture, notably Eric Gunnar Asplund's City Library in Stockholm, completed in 1928.

The tower and beacon stations use a tall, thin tower topped by a light above a low podium-type structure, combining elements developed in various new Dutch and German buildings. These are Holden's most successful attempt to add a feature to a station which could signal its presence from a distance. At Chiswick Park the tower had been bulky and had detracted from the appearance of the building.

Rather like the Northern Line stations, these uncompromisingly modern, almost industrial buildings, were situated in the contrasting surroundings of cosy and uninspiring suburbs. In that environment they made a very strong statement about the exciting nature of travel in general, and the Underground in particular.

Southgate, opened in 1933, is usually seen as the most individual of Holden's stations. Although it follows the circular form already used, it is unlike all the others. The booking hall is a low, circular building, with a totally glazed clerestory sitting on a drum of larger diameter, composed almost entirely of shops. The centre of the building is pierced by a column topped with an abstract illuminated finial. The general effect is that of a spaceship in the midst of suburban north London. A different building form entirely is the

Above: Winged wheel
sculptures by Joseph
Armitage on the façade
of Holden's Uxbridge
station, completed in
1938.

Top and right:
Cockfosters terminus by
Holden, 1933, was the
first of the concrete train
sheds. This station
contains some interesting
fittings such as the
formed timber platform
seating (top) and the
combined clock and
platform indicator
(right).

northern terminus of the Piccadilly Line at Cockfosters, also of 1933. This is basically a concrete version of the traditional iron and glass train shed, which conceals its size well from the outside. Holden repeated this form again at Uxbridge, the rebuilt western terminus completed in 1938 where he worked with L. H. Bucknell. Cockfosters is interesting in that it has some particularly well integrated fittings such as the formed timber platform seating between concrete supporting walls. At Uxbridge, decorative detailing such as a large heraldic stained-glass window by Ervin Bossanyi and two winged wheel sculptures on the exterior by Joseph Armitage were incorporated, both less controversial artistic additions than Epstein's work at 55 Broadway.

A number of stations in central London were rebuilt in the 1930s, incorporating

elements of the 'kit of parts' that constituted Holden's new Underground house style. Biscuit-coloured tiling, sometimes with contrasting colours or raised decorative details, bronze tubular handrails, clear Johnston-lettered signage on enamel panels in bronze wall frames or hanging lightboxes, and suspended globe lighting are all characteristic features of these stations. Free-standing 'passimeter' booking offices and new automatic ticket machines were also fitted, the latter being manufacturers' standard equipment encased in new simple blue metal boxes designed by Holden which had angled illuminated tops displaying destinations and fare values. New 'MH' type escalators were installed at these stations with Holden's bronze column uplighters on the incline and illuminated 'Way Out/To Trains' roundels in a complementary style at the top and bottom.

Above: Knightsbridge station booking hall, rebuilt in 1934, showing the free-standing 'passimeter' booking office and neat wall-mounted ticket machines.

Below: Moulded tile design by Harold Stabler, featuring 55 Broadway, 1938. A series of these with different designs appeared in new stations opened in 1939.

Right: Drawing and plan
of Warren Street station,
rebuilt in 1933–4. Pick
preferred to have station
designs presented to him
in sketch perspective
form rather than
technical drawings.

Far right: New escalators
at Holborn in 1933,
showing Holden's bronze
column uplighters which
were an attractive feature
of the Underground
until they were taken
out during the sixties.
The lights gave a sense
of drama to the escalator
shaft which has been
entirely lost with
overhead fluorescent
lighting. The uplighters
can still be seen at
Earls Court (Exhibition
entrance), Southgate and
St John's Wood.

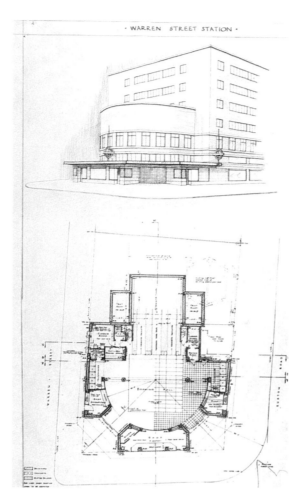

· WARREN STREET STATION ·

Holborn, Leicester Square and Warren Street
are all examples of stations given this
treatment which have since been extensively
refurbished. The Holden style is still
dominant, though in varying states of
preservation, at Knightsbridge, St Paul's,
Aldgate East and the exhibition end of Earls
Court, which has one of the few escalator sets
to retain its column uplighters.

The final flourish of what came to be seen
as the golden age of station architecture was
the 1935–40 New Works Programme, which
was interrupted by the war. This work was
not entirely under the control of Holden who
increasingly took on commissions outside
London Transport, notably the new London
University building in Bloomsbury. Much of
the responsibility for the construction fell to
Stanley Heaps, the company architect, who
successfully interpreted Holden's style at

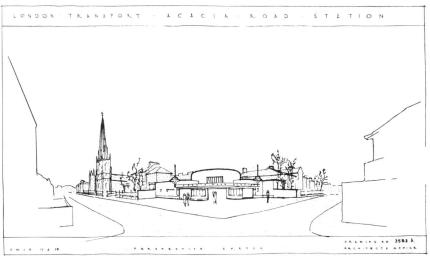

PARK ROYAL STATION, EALING. — Welch & lander. FF RIBA Architects, 58. Gloucester Place W.1.

As Holden took on commissions outside London Transport, he employed other architects to carry out his concepts. Pick was increasingly angry at this 'sub-contracting', even though the results were excellent.

Far left and top: St John's Wood, 1939, by Stanley Heaps, the London Transport staff architect. Acacia Road (top) was an early suggested name for this station.

Left: Park Royal by Welch and Lander, 1936. An original watercolour by the architects, who were also responsible for the adjacent shopping parade and housing estate.

St John's Wood and at the other new Bakerloo Line stations which opened in 1939. Other architects were also employed to carry out station commissions in the Holden style, notably Reginald Uren at Rayners Lane and Welch and Lander at Park Royal. Pick was furious at this apparent 'farming out' of the work, but it is clear that Holden was responsible for the initial concept in every case and that he oversaw all the schemes, including the work undertaken in-house by Heaps. As Adams, Holden and Pearson was a small architectural practice, this

Top: Uxbridge, 1938, by
Holden, working with
L.H. Bucknell; another
concrete train shed for
the western terminus of
the Piccadilly Line.

Above: East Finchley, also
by Holden and Bucknell,
1941, showing the
concrete lamp standards
incorporating the station
name, roundel and poster
boards which were
unfortunately replaced

in the 1980s. The statue
of an archer (right) is
by Eric Aumonier.
The arrow is being fired
towards Central London
symbolising the
Underground's speed and
directness.

sub-contracting was probably unavoidable given the amount of work London Transport required at this time.

Holden had not entirely finished with the Underground, however. Working with L. H. Bucknell he designed Uxbridge (1938) and East Finchley (1941) and, on his own, Wanstead, Gants Hill and Redbridge, all completed after the war in 1947. At East Finchley he used a number of ideas tried out elsewhere: round-ended waiting rooms with built-in wooden seating, flat concrete canopies also with rounded ends, and concrete lamp standards incorporating station nameboard roundels and poster boards. The building also had biscuit tiles applied to the lower two-thirds of the concrete canopy supports – a curious idea that detracts from the architectural form. Above the road bridge is a large art deco sculpture of an archer by Eric Aumonier, who had worked on 55 Broadway. This makes a dramatic statement about the speed and directness of the Underground as it fires its arrow towards Central London.

Of the later group of stations the most dramatic is at Gants Hill where, at the foot of the escalators, a lofty concourse was built between the platforms. This became known as the 'Moscow Hall' because of its resemblance to the Russian Metro stations on which London Transport engineers and their Moscow counterparts had co-operated. Pick had apparently liked the idea and had wanted to use a similar design in London. The success of the space is due to its simplicity and lack of clutter. The barrel-vaulted ceiling is lit both by uplighters and strip lighting, giving an airy feel to a subterranean space. It would, however, be of more practical use at a busier station: the main purpose of this layout in Moscow is to facilitate descent and ascent from the platforms by large crowds via escalators at both ends of the concourse. The three Central Line stations at Wanstead, Gants Hill and Redbridge were the last works that Holden undertook for the Underground.

It is all too easy to see the Holden-designed stations of the 1920s and 1930s as typical

Left: The 'Moscow Hall' at Gants Hill, designed by Holden in the late 1930s but not completed, because of the war, until 1947.

Above: Wood Green station platform, 1932, showing Holden's subtle use of concealed and reflected lighting.

Right: Chiswick Park booking hall by Holden, 1932, showing the use of natural light and strategically sited spaces for poster display at the street entrances.

of their period, but this was not so in the national context. Holden's designs were truly revolutionary and exploited space and light in a way that had not been considered for underground railway buildings and was certainly not matched by new stations for the main-line railways at the time. He deliberately used double-height spaces illuminated by natural light, to give an impression of space and airiness to a mode of transport that is by its nature cramped, and in most cases deprived of natural light. The feeling of light is very important to a passenger who may have some apprehension about travelling underground. Holden's careful use of reflected and concealed lighting on escalators, corridors and platforms gave these underground areas a welcoming glow which has been lost in the high-illumination fluorescent schemes used since the 1950s. The two-storey structure has another use in that at night, when fully illuminated, it serves as a powerful marketing tool for the Company's services. This was something that Pick, as a commercial man, never lost sight of, but which his successors failed to appreciate when a new generation of stations was designed thirty years later.

Opposite top: Newbury
Park bus station by
Oliver Hill, winner of the
1951 Festival of Britain
Architectural Prize.

Opposite far right:
St Albans country bus
station by Wallis, Gilbert
and Partners, 1936. The
adjacent bus garage by
the same architects was
closed in the 1980s.

Opposite near right: The
first of Holden's standard
bus shelter designs,
installed at Shannon
Corner, Malden, 1933.
Armrests are provided,
which are particularly
helpful for older people
who have difficulty
getting out of seats. This
simple aid disappeared
from later shelters.

Below: Hanger Lane
station by Lewis and
Curtis, 1948, a post-war
development of Holden's
style.

Architecture after Pick

Frank Pick left London Transport in 1940 and died the following year. Holden was never again commissioned by the Company. After Pick's departure and the transfer of power to department heads, it was inevitable that things would change. However, some of the first stations built after the war were very good. White City, designed by London Transport architect Kenneth Seymour in 1947, has simplicity and clarity in the best Holden tradition, with a spacious ticket hall, good use of brick, and some excellent bench-seat roundels. If it did not integrate commercial aspects very well into the booking hall, it has to be remembered that the station was built to serve one of the sites used for the 1948 Olympics, and therefore to handle enormous crowds at irregular intervals, rather than the high-street shopper. Among the other stations of the immediate post-war period, Hanger Lane, built by Lewis and Curtis in 1948 with a circular booking hall capped by a continuous clerestory, is quite successful.

Two of the most interesting buildings built during this time are not stations, although one was connected to a station. Newbury Park, an undistinguished Underground station on the Central Line, is dwarfed by a spectacular bus station canopy by Oliver Hill. This great hangar-like building of precast concrete won Hill the 1951 Festival of Britain architectural award. Although the bus station design is bold and imaginative, the relationship with the station is not particularly happy.

The second building of note is Stockwell Bus Garage of 1952, an enormous arched concrete construction by Adie Button and Partners which manages to dwarf the vehicles it was built to house and yet not dominate its surroundings. It is entirely unequivocal in design and entirely 'fit for purpose'. Ever since the Underground Group's takeover of the London General Omnibus Company, buses and bus infrastructure had been part of the organisation's responsibilities. Where possible, bus stations and turning points had been incorporated into new Underground station complexes as at Turnpike Lane, Southgate and Uxbridge or, in the country area, linked with new bus garages as at St Albans, Windsor and Dorking. The series of new country bus garages completed in the 1930s were all by Wallis, Gilbert and Partners, who produced variants on the Holden brick style for London Transport's road services. The same architects had been responsible for the extravagant art deco façades of the Hoover and Firestone factories in west London and for Victoria Coach Station, but had clearly been instructed by Pick to come up with something more restrained and domestic in appearance to suit country towns just outside London. These unassuming but thoughtfully designed buildings were transferred out of London Transport ownership when the Green Line and Country Bus services were hived off to the National Bus Company in 1970. Most have since been closed and sold off for redevelopment.

London Transport had also turned its attention to bus shelters and stops. In 1919 the first experimental bus stop had appeared on the streets, to universal acclaim – for the idea if not the design. Pick, who believed above all else in simplicity, saw that this was an opportunity to use the roundel symbol to signify bus service provision as it had been used earlier to denote rail services, but it took nearly twenty years to institute a complete network of stops throughout the London Transport area.

The standard bus shelters designed by Holden in the early 1930s were simple steel structures surmounted by roundels. A variety of types were tried – rectangular, round, and a miniature stadium type with a sloping roof. Most were uncompromising, and not always liked by the local councils in whose districts

they were sited. For rural locations, a series of very different wooden rustic designs with a pitched roof were devised. These were supplied by a timber building company called Astolat of Guildford. Sixty years on, the same London Transport shelter designs are still available in the Astolat catalogue, together

Previous pages: Stockwell
Garage by Adie Button
and Partners, 1952, a
concrete cathedral for
buses. This is the most
modern London
Transport structure to
be 'listed' by the
Department of National
Heritage for protection
and preservation.

with a simplified design created for London
Transport in the 1950s by the architect and
designer Jack Howe.

During the 1950s and early 1960s London
Transport built little of lasting interest. Some
work was done to Notting Hill Gate station
where a new booking hall was created with a
totally different feel. Influenced by the design
ethos of the Festival of Britain, it had a
chequer tile floor and a curved ticket office
façade with overstated detailing in aluminium

and steel. The new escalators were also clad
in aluminium instead of wood. What had
been lost was a sense of light and space, for
although the booking hall is generous in

size, the stark fluorescent lighting and the
flat ceiling emphasise the feeling of being
underground.

During the 1960s, the Victoria Line, the
first new tube railway for half a century, was
planned and built. In architectural terms, the
Victoria Line is as far as one can get from the
light, airy spaces of the Piccadilly Line, and
yet the design owed much to the Pick/Holden
era. The platforms were simply treated with
plain tiled walls and paving-slab floors; seats
and illuminated roundels were built in;
everything was ordered and fit for purpose.

The platform designs, which were done
as a total entity by Misha Black of the Design
Research Unit, have been criticised since
for being dull and lifeless; this probably had
as much to do with the lighting as with the
designs. The lighting was exposed fluorescent
tube with no relief for the eye, and there
was no attempt to bring natural light into
any of the circulation spaces. The general
ambience was not helped by the use of grey
and light blue throughout, which creates
a hard, clinical look.

The platform seating alcoves were backed
with tile motifs depicting some area of local
interest. These restrained decorations by well-
known artists such as Edward Bawden were
in some ways the most successful attempt to
bring a 'sense of place' to the underground
environment. Later attempts were generally
less restrained and tended to tell the story
at the expense of architectural form and
passenger information. There were very few
above-ground structures and they were
generally of poor quality. Blackhorse Road by
Kenneth Seymour, the staff architect, and the
little classical building over the vent shaft in
Gibson Square, Islington by Quinlan Terry,
are the best, but the opportunity to advertise
the railway by creating worthwhile surface
buildings was ignored.

A reaction to the austerity of the Victoria
Line can be seen in the designs for the Jubilee

Opposite (top): Notting Hill Gate booking hall by London Transport Architects, 1959–60, showing its 'Festival of Britain' design influence.

(bottom): Stockwell station platform, Victoria Line, by London Transport Architects and Design Research Unit, 1971. A well integrated design, with clean lines and tiled murals.

Left: Victoria Line ventilation shaft by Quinlan Terry, 1969. This little building in Gibson Square, Islington was almost the only surface building of any distinction on the Victoria Line. Linocut by Quinlan Terry.

Right: A watercolour study for the mosaic panel at the Oxford Street entrance to Tottenham Court Road station by Eduardo Paolozzi, 1984. The liberal use of mosaics throughout the refurbished station was a brave but unsuccessful attempt to give the station a 'sense of place'.

Line, opened in 1979. This line, which used additional platforms at existing stations, failed to arrive at any conclusions about a design style. A variety of decorative motifs are employed, ranging from the coy at Green Park to the purely illustrative at Charing Cross. In almost every case the decoration adds little to the experience of travel and says nothing about London Transport's corporate identity

the platforms with murals, but for the booking hall which uses a suspended vertical slat ceiling, interspersed with fluorescent lighting exposing the slab above. The ticket windows are of brightly coloured moulded fibreglass, a material that was in very common use at the time. The effect is not unpleasant, but the atmosphere is more that of a nightclub than a station, and the fibreglass has not lasted well.

or purpose. At Bond Street, for example, the tube station was almost completely submerged by a garish new shopping complex. One new feature tried out on the Jubilee Line was the use of yellow bands across the platform tunnel to signify the exits, a good idea that never became popular.

The most distinctive station on the line is Charing Cross, not only for the decoration of

Rather better than the Jubilee Line is the work done at the same time to extend the Piccadilly Line to Heathrow. The one totally new station with surface buildings, Hatton Cross, is clean and functional, as is Heathrow Terminals 1, 2, 3. Both use platform decorations relating to air travel. The later Terminal 4 station by London Underground architects (1986) is even better. It uses good quality materials and has well thought-out detailing with built-in seats and concealed lighting.

This restrained and confident work was in total contrast to the modernisation of the central area stations in the 1980s. The modernisation programme was an attempt to make stations more attractive to passengers in the belief that this could increase ridership. Each station was themed, rather like the Victoria Line in concept, though not in

Above: Charing Cross Northern Line platform, 1979, decorated with enlarged wood engravings by David Gentleman. This is one of the few decorative schemes that worked well, principally because the integrity of the design was not compromised by later additions such as airventing panels and advertising.

Left: Charing Cross Jubilee Line platform showing the yellow tunnel bands to signify exits, 1979.

Above: Heathrow Terminal 4 by London Underground Architects, 1986.

Right: Concorde motif by Tom Eckersley at Heathrow Terminals 1, 2, 3, 1977.

execution. Platforms, cross passages and staircases were subjected to decorative treatment by a variety of artists and designers, with consequently variable results. Charing Cross by David Gentleman is probably the most successful, being confined to the platform walls and treated as a single continuous work of art without disfiguring advertising or information panels. The mosaic designs at Tottenham Court Road by Eduardo Paolozzi have fared less well and are lost in a welter of additions.

Looking back on this programme of works it is clear that responding to fashionable ideas rather than keeping in mind the purpose of the building, and the purpose of the company, is likely to bring only transitory success, and to result in designs that are in some cases bound to date badly. It also shows the value of having a

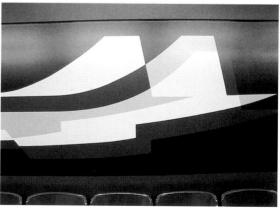

strategy for the use of art, to ensure that it does not dominate the perception of the building, and that it is used with a clear idea about how it is to fit in with commercial imperatives such as advertising and vending. Tottenham Court Road is a salutary lesson in how a promising public art commission can go badly wrong if the concept is not properly thought through.

Above: New Hillingdon station by Cassidy Taggart, 1993.

Left: New booking hall at Liverpool Street by London Underground Limited Architects, 1992. Restrained decoration and large open spaces make this a very successful scheme, which was carried out at the same time as the reconstruction of the main-line terminus above.

Above and right:
Hammersmith District
and Piccadilly Line
station rebuilt to the
designs of Minale
Tattersfield and Partners,
1993. Steel and glass
platform canopies
(right) provide a light,
airy environment
in the middle of the
Hammersmith Centre
West development. The
ticket hall with its
clerestory windows (top)
echoes Holden's work.

A Return to Fitness for Purpose

Since the mid-1980s, London Transport has spent some time reappraising its design policies. One of the immediate results of this is the changed attitude to environmental design and a return to the concepts of clarity and simplicity. During the period 1986–94 three new stations and two new bus stations have been designed and built. The stations cover two different types, one deep-tube at Angel, and two surface stations at Hammersmith and Hillingdon, but all have in common a return to simple forms, honesty in the use of materials and a preoccupation with fitness for purpose that Pick would have recognised and admired.

Both Hammersmith and Hillingdon make extensive use of glass canopies bringing as much natural light on to the platforms as possible, and at Hammersmith there is a

welcome return to clerestory windows in the ticket hall. Angel is the first of a new generation of rebuilt deep-level tubes and is notable for its simplicity, quality of materials and ordered approach. Whether these stations will be influential remains to be seen.

Concurrently with the Underground stations a new generation of bus infrastructure is being conceived in the 1990s. New bus

stations have recently been completed at Harrow, Hammersmith and Stratford. These designs herald a different approach to bus passengers who have too long been treated as second-class citizens by London Transport. The bus stations now provide a range of facilities such as vending, telephones and information. Although neither Harrow nor Hammersmith is exceptionally good architecture, the design of the interior spaces makes life as convenient and comfortable as possible. Stratford is a rather more ambitious tented structure, as yet unproven but already giving a focus and sense of drama to an area of visual confusion previously dominated by its dreary and unattractive buildings.

Much effort has also been expended in recent years in the design of bus shelters to give greater comfort and protection. The designs produced by Kenneth Grange of Pentagram for the London Transport/Adshel partnership are a distinguished addition to the London street scene. To complement these, a new generation of bus stops has been designed by John Elson and is slowly being installed. Using aluminium section instead of concrete posts, they are able to act as conduit for cables and therefore provide lighting for timetables and boarding diagrams, a much-needed improvement. They will also be able to incorporate electronic displays showing the waiting time for the next bus.

During the late 1980s and early 1990s, London Transport had an involvement in the new light railway built to help the regeneration of Docklands. The work was done as a low cost design and build package by GEC/Mowlem and was extremely basic, providing short platform canopies on elevated sections of track to serve the computer-

Above: Concept sketch for Stratford Bus Station by London Transport Architects, 1994, part of the programme of upgrading and improving bus passenger facilities. Illustration by Bruce Gornick.

Above and right: The Docklands Light Railway was owned and operated by London Transport from 1987–92. During that time it commissioned Ahrends Burton and Koralek to design the stations on the extension to Beckton. The light modern structures are entirely appropriate for their purpose and fit well into the emerging Docklands townscape. The extension opened in 1993.

controlled driverless trains. London Transport was not directly involved in the design of the first part of the railway but was given the operation to run for a short time when it opened in 1987, before it was transferred to the London Docklands Development Corporation in 1992. Whilst London

completely integrated design, they are in some ways direct successors to Holden's work.

In 1988 London Transport was given Victoria Coach Station after the break up of the National Bus Company. Although London Transport had no responsibility for such services, they were clearly under some

Transport had responsibility for the operation, it commissioned the design and construction of the extension to Beckton, for which the chosen architects were Ahrends Burton and Koralek. The designs are elegant and distinctive, using durable and largely vandal-proof materials at unstaffed stations in areas where there is little local infrastructure or community. With bright lift towers and crisply detailed elements contributing to a

obligation to modernise the operation of the Coach Station, which looked like some of the District Line stations before the Holden/Pick era. Signage was chaotic, the facilities were primitive and the coaches and people were intermixed in a distinctly dangerous way. London Transport appointed designers Jenkins Group to completely modernise and refurbish the 1930s building. The result is a transformation into something approaching an air terminal. Passenger facilities are excellent, and the passenger operation has been rationalised to separate people and coaches. The new design has already won several design awards. Although not in the mainstream of London Transport business, it is a striking example of how business determination coupled with enlightened and intelligent design can transform even the worst operation.

Above and left: Victoria Coach Station. A refurbishment by Jenkins Group in 1993 changed the primitive environment (left) that London Transport inherited into a facility on a par with an airport terminal.

In 1993 the go-ahead was given for the long-delayed extension of the Jubilee Line south of the river and then back into Docklands. The design approach has been to take each station as a separate entity, with a different architect appointed for each one, and to use the best architects possible. Although each of the chosen architects works within what might loosely be described as the 'high-tech modern' style, each is providing a very different solution. The line will therefore have less cohesion than perhaps it should, but each station will be individually interesting.

Whether the approach will be successful remains to be seen, but the initial designs by Michael Hopkins for Westminster and Norman Foster for Canary Wharf look particularly challenging and exciting.

A different approach is being taken with the proposed CrossRail scheme which is intended to run under London from Paddington to Liverpool Street and above ground west to Reading and east to Shenfield. It will be an underground railway to main-line dimensions so that standard size rolling stock can be used, and will have interchange with the Underground but be physically separate from it, a concept similar to the suburban link lines that were built under Paris in the 1970s. The design approach being taken here is to appoint one team to do running tunnels and platforms, and to treat the ticket halls as part of the development above – each again designed by different architects. The idea of combining continuity of experience below ground with bold architectural statement above is an interesting concept and some very exciting proposals have been produced, notably by Alsop & Stormer at Paddington.

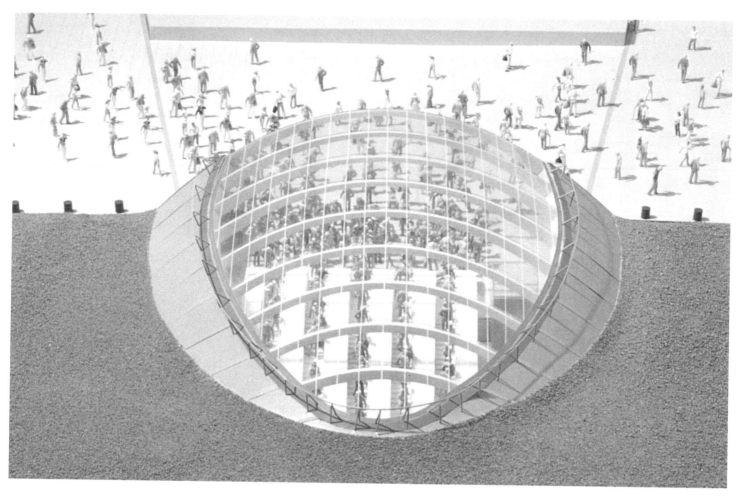

In recent years major capital projects such as new Underground lines and station reconstructions have been persistently delayed or abandoned because of a lack of Government funding. The Jubilee Line is finally under way and will now be completed before the turn of the century, but at the time of writing, CrossRail's future is still in the balance. Nevertheless, even if only some of the schemes are carried out, it is clear that London is set to gain some of the best new transport architecture and design since the golden age of Pick and Holden's collaboration in the pre-war period.

Above: Canary Wharf station by Norman Foster & Partners. Two views of one of the exciting designs for the new Jubilee Line extension.

Opposite: Paddington station CrossRail design scheme by Alsop & Stormer. This proposal for the west London gateway station brings natural light down on to the station in a great slit trench with a glazed roof. A dramatic statement that epitomises the concept of a railway under London for the 21st century.

Further Reading

The outstanding qualities of London Transport design have been widely acclaimed for over sixty years and yet there have been very few good accounts or analyses of it. Inevitably the most detailed studies have been of vehicles and rolling stock, although these tend to concentrate heavily on technical developments and service histories with little consideration of design.

Many of the most useful studies have been in magazine articles, some of which are included here. This is not an exhaustive list of references, but provides pointers for those wishing to investigate London Transport design history more fully. All of these works should be available for consultation, by appointment, in the London Transport Museum Library (0171 379 6344). Photographs, films, posters and other printed material can also be consulted by researchers.

The Design Context

Christian Barman, *The Things We See, Public Transport* (Penguin Books, 1949)
Lewis Blackwell, *Twentieth Century Type* (Laurence King, 1992)
Avril Blake, *Misha Black* (Design Council, 1984)
John and Avril Blake, *The Practical Idealists, A History of Design Research Unit* (Lund Humphries, 1969)
W.P.N. Edwards, *A Note on Contemporary Architecture in Northern Europe* (The Pick/Holden tour of 1930, printed for private circulation by London Underground, 1931)
Adrian Forty, *Objects of Desire, Design and Society 1750-1980* (Thames and Hudson, 1986)
Jonathan Glancey, *Douglas Scott* (Design Council, 1988)
Jennifer Hawkins and Marianne Hollis (eds), *Thirties, British Art and Design Before the War* (Arts Council, 1979)
Richard Hollis, *Graphic Design, A Concise History* (Thames and Hudson, 1994)
Frederique Huygen, *British Design, Image and Identity* (Thames and Hudson, 1989)
Eitan Karol and Finch Allibone, *Charles Holden, Architect 1875-1960* (RIBA, 1988)

Lance Knobel, *The Faber Guide to Twentieth Century Architecture, Britain and Northern Europe* (Faber and Faber, 1985)
Fiona MacCarthy, *British Design Since 1880* (Lund Humphries, 1982)
Fiona MacCarthy and Patrick Nuttgens, *Eye for Industry, Royal Designers for Industry 1936-1986* (Lund Humphries/RSA, 1986)
Liz McQuiston and Barry Kitts, *Graphic Design Source Book* (Chartwell Books, 1987)
Nikolaus Pevsner, *Studies in Art, Architecture and Design, Victorian and After* (Thames and Hudson, 1968)

London Transport History and Design

Anon., 'Improving London's Transport' (*The Railway Gazette*, 1946)
Anon., 'Underground Extensions and Improvements' (*Railway Gazette Supplement*, 18 November 1932)
Theo Barker, *Moving Millions, A Pictorial History of London Transport* (London Transport Museum, 1990)
Theo Barker and Michael Robbins, *A History of London Transport Vol. One: The Nineteenth Century* (Allen and Unwin, 1963)
Vol. Two: The Twentieth Century to 1970 (Allen and Unwin, 1974)
[Vol. Two includes an appendix listing all published articles by Frank Pick]
Christian Barman, *The Man Who Built London Transport, A Biography of Frank Pick* (David and Charles, 1979)
Piers Connor, *Underground Official Handbook* (Capital Transport, 1990)
Desmond F. Croome and Alan A. Jackson, *Rails Through the Clay, A History of London's Tube Railways* (Capital Transport, 1993)
Norbert Dutton, 'Living Design, London Transport' (*Art and Industry*, Vol.41, No. 244, October 1946)
John Glover, *London's Underground* (Ian Allan, 1991)
Oliver Green, *The London Underground, An Illustrated History* (Ian Allan, 1988)
Oliver Green and John Reed, *The London Transport Golden Jubilee Book* (Daily Telegraph, 1983)

Corin Hughes Stanton, 'Design Management, Pioneering Policies' (*Design Magazine*, 197, May 1965)
Alan A. Jackson, *London's Metropolitan Railway* (David and Charles, 1986)
O. S. Nock, *Underground Railways of the World* (A & C Black, 1973)
Sheila Taylor, *A Journey Through Time, London Transport Photographs 1880-1965* (Laurence King, 1992)
J. P. Thomas, *Handling London's Underground Traffic* (London Underground, 1928)

Buses

Ken Blacker, *RT, The Story of a London Bus* (Capital Transport, 1979)
Ken Blacker, *Routemaster, Vol. One, 1954-1969* (Capital Transport, 1991)
J. Graeme Bruce and Colin Curtis, *The London Motor Bus* (London Transport, 1977)
Colin Curtis, *Buses of London* (London Transport, 1979)
John R. Day, *The Story of the London Bus* (London Transport, 1973)
A. A. M. Durrant, *Aldenham Works, Large Scale Bus Overhaul* (London Transport, 1956)
Ken Glazier, *RF* (Capital Transport, 1991)
Charles E. Lee, *The Horse Bus as a Vehicle* (London Transport, 1974)
Charles E. Lee, *The Early Motor Bus* (London Transport, 1974)
Gavin Martin, *London Buses 1929-1939* (Ian Allan, 1990)
John Reed, *London Buses Past and Present* (Capital Transport, 1994)
George Robbins and B. J. Atkinson, *The London B Type Motor Omnibus* (World of Transport, 1991)
George Robbins and Alan Thomas, *London Buses Between the Wars* (Marshall, Harris and Baldwin, 1980)
Alan Townsin, *The Best of British Buses No. 6 AEC Regals* (Transport Publishing Co., 1982)
No. 7 AEC Regents 1929-42 (Transport Publishing Co., 1982)
Alan Townsin, *Bus Profile, Routemaster* (Ian Allan, 1990)

Trams and Trolleybuses

Ken Blacker, *Trolleybus*
(Capital Transport, 1978)
John R. Day, *London's Trams and Trolleybuses*
(London Transport, 1977)
E. R. Oakley, *LCC Tramways Vol. One: South
London Vol. Two: North London*
(London Tramways History
Group/TLRS/LRTA, 1989 and 1991)
C. S. Smeeton, *Metropolitan Electric Tramways
Vols. One and Two*
(LRTA/TLRS, 1984 and 1986)
D. W. Willoughby and E. R. Oakley,
London Transport Tramways Handbook
(Nemo Productions, 1972)

Underground Trains

Anon., 'Central Line Trains, The Quiet
Revolution'
(*Modern Railways Magazine,* July 1994)
J. Graeme Bruce,
The London Underground, Tube Stock
(Ian Allan, 1988)
J. Graeme Bruce, *Steam to Silver*
(Capital Transport, 1983)
J. Graeme Bruce and Piers Connor,
Underground Train Overhaul
(Capital Transport, 1991)
Piers Connor, *The 1938 Tube Stock*
(Capital Transport, 1989)
Brian Hardy, *London Underground Rolling Stock*
(Capital Transport, 1993)
Brian Hardy, *LPTB Rolling Stock 1933-1948*
(Bradford Barton, 1981)

Information and Publicity

Anon., *Art for All, London Transport Posters
1908-1949*
(Art and Technics, 1949)
Christian Barman, *The Writing on the Wall*
(London Transport Staff Meetings Session,
1937-1938)
Tim Demuth, *The Johnston Story*
(*London Bus Magazine,* Vols. 34 and 36,
1980-1981)
Ken Garland, *Mr Beck's Underground Map*
(Capital Transport, 1994)
Oliver Green, *Underground Art, London
Transport Posters 1908 to the Present*
(Studio Vista, 1990)
Oliver Green, *Metro-land*
(London Transport Museum/Oldcastle
Books, 1987; reprint of 1932 edition)

Mark Haworth Booth, *E. McKnight Kauffer,
A Designer and His Public*
(Gordon Fraser, 1979)
Harold F. Hutchison, *London Transport Posters*
(London Transport, 1963)
Michael F. Levey, *London Transport Posters*
(Phaidon/London Transport, 1976)
Jonathan Riddell and William T. Stearn,
By Underground to Kew
(Studio Vista, 1994)
Jonathan Riddell and Peter Denton,
By Underground to the Zoo
(Studio Vista, 1995)

London Transport Architecture

Anon., *Changing Stations, A Review of Recent
London Underground Station Design by LUL's
Architectural Services and their Consultants*
(LUL Architectural Services, 1993)
Walter Bayes, 'Sense and Sensibility,
The New Head Offices of the
Underground Railways'
(*The Architectural Review,* November 1929)
Richard Cork, *Art Beyond the Gallery in Early
20th-century England*
(Yale University Press, 1985)
Richard Cork (ed.),
Eduardo Paolozzi Underground
(Royal Academy of Arts, 1986)
Brian Hanson, 'Singing The Body Electric
with Charles Holden'
(*The Architectural Review,* December 1975)
David Lawrence, *Underground Architecture*
(Capital Transport, 1994)
David Leboff, *London Underground Stations*
(Ian Allan, 1994)
Laurence Menear, *London's Underground
Stations*
(Midas Books, 1983)
Grahame Middleton, 'Charles Holden and
his London Underground Stations'
(*Architectural Association Quarterly,* Vol. 8,
No.2, 1976)
Alan Powers (ed), *End of the Line? The Future
of London Underground's Past*
(Victorian Society/Thirties Society, 1987)

Key Dates

The following are the key dates in the history of London Transport and the organisations responsible for public transport in London which preceded it.

1829

First horse bus service introduced between Paddington and the Bank, via the Angel, by George Shillibeer.

1855

A French company, the Compagnie Générale des Omnibus de Londres, started to purchase most of London's small-scale horse bus proprietors. The combine began operating in Britain, as the London General Omnibus Company (LGOC), in 1856.

1861

First horse tramway, built by an American, George Francis Train, along the Bayswater Road from Marble Arch to Porchester Terrace. (Because of the disruption caused to other road users by the raised rails, it was soon removed.)

1863

The Metropolitan Railway – the first Underground line in the world – opened, on 10 January between Paddington (Bishop's Road) and Farringdon Street, with steam-hauled trains. (Now forms part of the Hammersmith and City Line.)

1870

New horse tram routes (with rails sunk into the road surface) opened between Bow Church and Whitechapel Church, and between Brixton Station and Kennington Church.

1890

Opening of the City & South London Railway between King William Street and Stockwell – the first deep-level electric 'tube' railway in the world. (Now forms part of the Northern Line.)

1901

Opening of the first electric tramways, in west London, by the London United Tramways (LUT).

1902

Incorporation of the Underground Electric Railways Company of London (known as the Underground Group), which initially comprised the District Railway, the projected Bakerloo, Piccadilly and Hampstead tube lines, and LUT.

1905

Electrification of District Railway and inner sections of the Metropolitan Railway.

1910

The first mass-produced motorbus (the B type) introduced by the LGOC.

1912

The Underground Group acquired financial control of the LGOC, which at this period was purchasing or merging with other bus companies to produce a virtual LGOC monopoly by 1914.

1913

The Underground Group acquired control of the Central London and City & South London Railways.

1914

Last horse bus.

1915

Last horse tram.

1929

Opening by the Underground Group of 55 Broadway, now London Transport's headquarters offices.

1930

Express 'Green Line' coach routes introduced.

1931

Trolleybuses introduced by LUT in the Kingston area, replacing trams.

1933

London Passenger Transport Board (LPTB) established (from 1 July) with powers to take over and operate all bus, tram, trolleybus and Underground railway services in London and adjacent counties. It was soon known simply as London Transport.

1947

Transport Act established the British Transport Commission, responsible to the Minister of Transport (with effect from 1 January 1948). London Transport formed a constituent part of the Commission.

1952

London's last tram ran from Woolwich to New Cross on the night of 5/6 July.

1962

London's last trolleybus ran from Wimbledon to Fulwell on the night of 8/9 May.

1968–9

First new Underground line since 1907 – the Victoria Line – opened, with trains operating automatically.

1969

The Transport (London) Act created the London Transport Executive, responsible to the Greater London Council. The Act provided for the transfer of the bus and coach services in areas outside Greater London to London Country Bus Services, a subsidiary of the National Bus Company. These changes came into effect on 1 January 1970.

1984

London Regional Transport (LRT) set up on 29 June, responsible to the Secretary of State for Transport.

1985

London Buses Limited and London Underground Limited established as operating subsidiaries of LRT.

1986

Tendering of bus routes in London began.

1987

Docklands Light Railway opened, linking the Isle of Dogs to Stratford and to the City (at Tower Gateway), with trains operating automatically.

1990

LRT became known again as London Transport for all but legal purposes.

1992

Docklands Light Railway transferred to the London Docklands Development Corporation.

1994

Privatisation of London Buses companies began.

Key to Endpapers

1	6	11	16	21	26	31	36
2	7	12	17	22	27	32	37
3	8	13	18	23	28	33	38
4	9	14	19	24	29	34	39
5	10	15	20	25	30	35	40